RVs
Getting Out and STAYING Out

Alan & Barbara Lidstone

Fulcrum Publishing
Golden, Colorado

Library of Congress Cataloging-in-Publication Data

Lidstone, Alan.
RVs—getting out and staying out / Alan and Barbara Lidstone.
    p. cm.
Includes index.
ISBN 1-55591-312-1 (pbk.)
1. Recreational vehicle living. 2. Recreational vehicles.
I. Lidstone, Barbara. II. Title.
TX1110.L53 2001
643'.2—dc21

2001002337

Printed in the United States of America
0 9 8 7 6 5 4 3 2 1

Editorial: Erin A. Lawson, Daniel Forrest-Bank
Cover and interior design: Michelle Taverniti
Interior formatting: Rosanne Pignone, Pro Production
Cover photograph: Recreational Vehicle in Zion National Park, copyright © Gunter Marx/CORBIS.

Fulcrum Publishing
16100 Table Mountain Parkway, Suite 300
Golden, Colorado 80403
(800) 992-2908 · (303) 277-1623
www.fulcrum-books.com

CONTENTS

INTRODUCTION 7

SECTION 1—GETTING ON THE ROAD 13

Chapter 1—How to Find the Information You Need 14

Campground Directories and Guides, 15

User Groups, 16

Discount Cards, 21

Equipment, Parts, Service, and Supplies, 22

Interstate Exit Guides and Truck Stop Guides, 24

Mountain Directories, 25

RV Website Addresses and Information Links, 26

Chapter 2—Trip Planning That Works 31

Choosing Your Destinations, 32

Traveling with the Support of an RV Group, 34

Planning Each Stop, 35

Making Reservations, 36

Trip Routing Considerations, 37

Safety Considerations, 38

Scheduling RV Service While on the Road, 39

The All-Important Trip Book, 39

Building the RV Library, 40

RVs, Computers, and the Internet, 42

Powering a Computer in an RV, 43

Internet Service Providers, 45

Chapter 3—Making the Trip Comfortable 47

Local Transportation and Towing, 47

I Want My Big Refrigerator!, 54

Entertainment Media, 55

Privacy and Climate Control, 59

Weathering the Storm, 59

Dispatching the Laundry, 61

Computing on the Road, 63

Taking Your Medicine, 65

Cool- and Cold-Weather RVing, 68

Chapter 4—Visiting National, State, and County Parks 73

National Parks, 73

National Parks and Federal Lands Websites and Telephone Numbers, 73

Discounted Entrance Fees for National Parks, 74

State Parks, 74

County Parks, 76

Chapter 5—Entering Canada and Mexico 77

Canada, 77

Mexico, 80

Chapter 6—Making Sure the RV Is Ready to Roll 84

RV Service Providers, 84

Types of RV Service, 86

Before You Hit the Road, 87

Don't Forget the RV Documents, 88

Chapter 7—What Goes in the RV? 89

Where Do You Put Everything?, 89

Loading Up, 90

What Else Goes in Besides Food and Clothing?, 92

Chapter 8—Closing Up the House 99

What to Do with the Telephone Service, 99

"Running the Household" Activities, 100

Inside the Home, 101

Outside the Home, 102

While You're Gone, 102

SECTION 2—STAYING OUT ON THE ROAD 103

Chapter 9—Banking, Money, and Bill Paying 104

Banking and Money, 104

Paying Bills, 108

Chapter 10—Keeping in Touch 112

On the Phone, 112

In Writing, 117

On the Internet, 120

Technology Wrap-Up, 128

Chapter 11—Driving 130

Driving Tips, 130

Things to Avoid While Driving an RV, 132

Chapter 12—How to Keep from Getting Lost 139

Road Atlases and Maps, 139

Free Trip Routing and Mapping Services, 139

Low-Cost Software Applications, 141

Powering Up Your GPS and Other Devices, 142

Low-Cost RV GPS Systems, 143

Mid-Range Navigation Systems, 144

High-End Navigation Systems, 146

Suggestions, 147

Chapter 13—Setting Up and Taking Down the RV Site 149

Positioning the RV, 149

Hooking Up Utilities, 150

Jacks/Air Bag Stabilizers and Slideouts, 155

Stove and Hot Water Heater, 157

Satellite TV, 157

TV Antenna, 158

The Awnings, 158

When It's Time to Head Out, 158

Chapter 14—Returning Home 162

On the Road, 162

Back at the House, 162

Securing the RV Until the Next Trip, 163

SECTION 3—RV SUPPORT AND SERVICES 165

**Chapter 15—Insurance, Road Service,
Warranty Coverage, and Medical Evacuation 166**

RV Insurance, 166

Road Service and Towing Service, 167

Warranty Services Included with the RV, 169

Extended Warranty Services, 170

Medical Evacuation and Assistance Services, 172

Chapter 16—Manuals and Other RV Documents 174

RV Manufacturer Documents, 175

Chassis and Power Train Documents, 176

Systems and Accessories Documents, 177

Generic Repair and Maintenance Manuals, 177

Obtaining Replacement Documents, 178

Organizing the Technical Documents, 178

Chapter 17—Preventive Maintenance 180

What Is Preventive Maintenance?, 181

Who Does Preventive Maintenance?, 181

What's the Difference Between
    Preventive and Scheduled Maintenance?, 181

Preventive Maintenance Actions and Tasks, 182

Scheduled and Major Maintenance Needs, 191

Chapter 18—Storing the RV over the Winter 194

Engine and Power Train, 195

Coach, 195

Fresh Water System, 197

Holding Tanks, 199

APPENDIX A—State Park Websites and Related Information 200

**APPENDIX B—Suggested Chassis and Power Train Preventive
Maintenance Checklist 215**

**APPENDIX C—Suggested Coach-Related Preventive Maintenance
Checklist 216**

APPENDIX D—Sample Checklist for Loading RV 219

INDEX 221

INTRODUCTION

We really want you to read this book before leaving for your first RV adventure. We know how excited you are; you've wanted to do it for years, and now you have the RV of your dreams.

We wouldn't trade RVing for any other type of vacation. We took the plunge into extended motorhome trips with excited anticipation and a determination to make sure we could stay out for as long as we wanted. We purchased our first motorhome in 1997—a used 1987, 28-foot Champion. We were immediately off and running for fun and education in the world of RVing.

Although the Champion had low mileage when we purchased it, it had been resting for several years and needed spiffing up and repairs. After a thorough inspection by Ed Cote's RV Storage and Service facility in Sarasota, Florida, we purchased it for a reasonable price. We came to understand and appreciate the technology of RVs as the repairs and upgrades were completed. The original cost plus the additional expenses needed to get the Champion into tip-top shape gave us an RV that we thoroughly enjoyed.

Before taking the RV out for the first time, Alan spent hours going through the owner's manual—without actually connecting any hoses or cords. Barbara put together a checklist to help ensure that needed supplies and clothing came along with us on the trip.

Our hands-on education began when we reached our first destination and began trying to set up our first RV site. The sewer hookup was not where Alan expected it to be, and locating the TV cable connection proved to be a bust. The friendly RVer staying in the next site came over and asked if the RV was new to us. He pointed out the cable connection and advised that we should look about 9 inches farther in from the side of the coach for the sewer hookup.

Our neighbor's friendliness and the prospect of visiting new and favorite haunts sold us on RVing quickly. We knew we were hooked after our first few trips around Florida because our trips became longer in both time and mileage. We ended up trading in the Champion for a pristine and peppy new 1998 Winnebago Chieftain.

Why We Wrote This Book

Like many other RVers, we spent most of our working years using our camping equipment and pop-up camper for weekend and holiday trips that never lasted more than a few weeks. As we neared retirement, we found ourselves with more free time. The idea of traveling in our RV for extended periods and over longer distances became more and more appealing. We looked forward to seeing many places we had read and heard about.

The idea of extended RVing seemed a bit overwhelming to us at first. Between the seemingly awesome and complex logistics of "living on the road" and the technology of the motorhome, we had much new information to absorb and master. The RV's many appliances and its equipment, electronics, and fittings seemed to need the talents of an electrician, engineer, and plumber all at once.

Fortunately, extended RV trips are easier now than in the past because today's motorhomes combine the functions and capabilities of a heavy-duty vehicle with the amenities and comforts of a complete home on wheels. Today's RVs can smoothly and comfortably travel on the Interstate Highway System at 70 miles per hour while towing a car. They can carry thousands of pounds of equipment, and they provide the living space and the personal, recreational, and support items that RVers need.

As we visited local RV dealers to check out various makes and models, we had the opportunity to tour many types of motorhomes, including fifth-wheels, recreational trailers, and tow vehicles. All were well designed and easily capable of providing safe, reliable recreational service for fifteen to twenty years or longer, when properly maintained.

Our greatest challenge did not lie in a search for reliable and well-built equipment. Instead, we had some difficulty selecting the RV we liked best from the many excellent and varied models available from several local dealers.

We also found that although there is a great deal of information published about RVing, all the bits and pieces of information we needed were spread out across dozens of books, websites, user groups, and other organizations. What we didn't find was a single definitive RV book that told us most of what we would need to know before and during trips so that we could make the most of this recreational lifestyle.

After three years of fun—and sometimes funny—RV trips of short, medium, and long duration, we decided to pull together our experiences, the experiences of other RVers, and the array of information about RVing we had acquired. The result is *RVs—Getting Out and STAYING Out.*

What We Hope You Will Take from Our Book

To the benefit of the entire RVing community, our book tries to share, in a single publication, our accumulated experiences and tips, as well as those of our RVing friends. We hope this book provides you with a starting point, a helpful overview of RVing, and useful information about available services and support. By sharing what we know, we aim to help RV owners and their families enjoy traveling on the road with ease, confidence, comfort, and peace of mind.

This book provides new and experienced RVers with a complete view of startup activities, planning, available resources, and RV maintenance. After reading our book, we hope you will be able to stay out for as long as desired and that you will have a better grasp of what it takes to keep a motorhome in good, safe, and reliable condition.

Our book will be of particular interest to RVers who would like to make extended trips of up to several months. And although we use the word "motorhome" throughout the book, much of the information provided applies to owners of fifth-wheels and recreational tow trailers as well. We attempt to give you the "what, where, and how" of short- and extended-trip RVing and to help you make the most of your invested time, effort, and money.

How Our Book Is Organized

Our book is organized into three sections: Getting on the Road, Staying Out on the Road, and RV Support and Services. We have found it useful to view the process of RVing as an exercise in "project management." Although all projects deliver some "one-two punches" in the form of unavoidable changes to plans, the best way to get into extended-trip RVing is always to plan ahead as much as possible. We hope to give you the means to deal with most problems that arise quickly, easily, and with minimum disruption.

Our checklists are a helpful part of the project management metaphor. For instance, completion of one task can trigger the start of the "attack" on the next. That's why we regard our checklists as must-haves. They provide us with a snapshot of to-do items that we consider important.

RVers use checklists for the same reason doctors, pilots, and technicians use them—to avoid unexpected and unwanted situations and to prevent delay and extra expenses. Checklists are invaluable because RVers sometimes have to do many tasks within a short time period. We are sure you will find our checklists helpful, but we hope you will customize them for your own needs.

In project management style, we prioritize to-do items based on the adverse consequences of missing a task. For instance, driving with the antenna raised may mean expenses of about $250 for installation of a new antenna and repair of minor roof damage. However, driving off with the awning down, the slideout extended, or the jacks down can cause substantial structural damage running into thousands of dollars for repairs. Such regrettable (but preventable!) incidents might also delay the start or continuation of your trip.

Checklists also help keep us from leaving behind small miscellaneous items—such as a coax cable for the TV connection or the water pressure regulator—as we pull out of a campground early in the morning. Each of these left-behind items may not cost much, but their combined cost might turn out to be a whopping expense over time.

We've told you what works for us so far. We will continue to learn more on each new trip, but we find that our experiences and the lessons we've learned in our first three years of RVing have worked out most of our kinks.

Once you've reached your first destination and put down your awning to enjoy a great view and the company of your RVing neighbors, we know you'll look forward to your future RV trips as much as we do. We hope this book will get you started faster, more confidently and comfortably, and as economically as possible. Happy RVing!

Getting on the Road

CHAPTER 1

HOW TO FIND THE INFORMATION YOU NEED

We will help you through the maze of mind-boggling and overwhelming RV information sources available by pointing you toward useful resources and helping you to select materials for your own RV library and knowledge base.

RV owners have access to a large amount of information and many service providers that make owning and operating an RV easier. Helpful information is available for easier trip planning, determining when and where to travel, and reducing the costs of RVing. RV publications are readily available from local and major bookstores, on-line bookstores, libraries, Camping World stores, and RV suppliers. In addition, there are quite a few internet sites dedicated to providing information and assistance to RVers.

Examples of some of the publications, services, and sources of information that help streamline RV trip planning and the trips themselves include:

- Campground directories and guides
- RV user groups
- RV discount cards
- RV equipment, parts, service, and supplies
- Road atlases
- Interstate exit guides and truck stop guides
- Repair and maintenance manuals
- Mountain directories
- RV website addresses and information links for RVers

These resources provide all the information and contacts you will need to maximize the use and enjoyment of your RV while making the most of the time and money you have invested.

Campground Directories and Guides

Campground directories provide extensive information regarding campgrounds, services, rates, and other resources on a state-by-state basis. In addition to campgrounds and resorts, the major directories also list RV repair and service facilities. Directories are available for campgrounds that are open to the public, open to members only, or limited to specific interest groups.

Examples of popular directories for campgrounds open to the public include:

- *Trailer Life Directory:* Campgrounds, RV Parks and Services, available from TL Enterprises; also available in CD-ROM format as Trailer Life RV Campground Finder.
- *Woodall's Campground Directories*, available from Woodall Publications Corp. in eastern, western, and North American versions.
- *Guide to Free Campgrounds*, available from Cottage Publications; lists thousands of free camping areas.
- *Anderson's Campground and RV Park Travel Directory:* covers the East Coast from Florida to northern New York.
- *AAA CampBooks*, available from AAA at no charge to members; this series of regional campground directories covers all fifty states.

The Trailer Life and Woodall's campground directories also contain excellent information regarding state laws affecting RVers, tourist and area attractions, and addresses and phone numbers of state recreational agencies. They are updated every year. Both of these directories are available for on-line viewing at their websites, which are listed at the end of this chapter.

The Trailer Life directory includes a listing of RV dump stations by state, as well as a separate set of listings for military campground facilities for active and retired military personnel.

Woodall also publishes regional newsletters that provide valuable information about campgrounds and services on a regional basis, as well as highly informative articles about RV care and maintenance. These newsletters are available at many campgrounds at no charge.

Many individual states publish campground directories that are available directly from the states (either through the internet or by contacting state departments of parks and tourism by mail or phone), at Interstate Highway System welcome stations and visitor centers, and at many individual campgrounds at no charge. A number of national private campground organizations, such as Kampgrounds of America (KOA) and Yogi Bear's Jellystone Park Camp-Resorts, publish their own national directories with descriptions of the campgrounds, local attractions, and state maps.

Military RV, Camping & Rec Areas Around the World, available from Military Living Publications, is a directory of campgrounds and recreational areas on military bases or facilities that are open to active and retired members of the armed forces and some active and retired employees of the U.S. Department of Defense.

We get the most useful and complete information by consulting multiple sources. The directories each carry different types of information, all of which is of interest to RVers. However, not all campgrounds are listed in all directories. Most of the campground directories are available on the Web (see the list at the end of this chapter) and provide the same campground and service-provider entries found in the printed versions. Sometimes, however, the on-line information is different from the information in the printed directories.

User Groups

RV user groups offer information, trip routing, rallies open to members, assistance, and a variety of RV services. They all have informative websites with links to other RV-related websites.

The RV user groups, such as Good Sam and Family Motor Coach Association, send their members excellent magazines (which are included with the price of membership) that provide timely and informative articles. Topics covered include the RV lifestyle, technical issues, RV resorts and campgrounds, pending RV-related legislation, and other subjects of interest to RVers. We unfailingly read our Good Sam *Highways* magazine cover-to-cover within two days of receiving it. It is one of our primary sources of information and provides very helpful hints and suggestions.

RV user groups also sponsor many rallies, including state rallies, for their members. In addition, they offer RV services such as discounts at selected campgrounds and resorts; local clubs and chapters; emergency road service; mail hold and forwarding service; long distance calling cards; extended RV warranties; medical air transportation; and health, home, and auto insurance.

RV user groups may be open to the general public, specific groups, owners of specific manufacturers' RVs, or to members of private campgrounds only.

Websites for a number of the user groups are provided at the end of this chapter.

RV User Groups Open to the General Public

These groups include:

- Good Sam
- Family Motor Coach Association (FMCA)
- Escapees RV Club—for full-timers
- Family Campers and RVers (FCRV)
- Family Travel Trailer Association—for fifth-wheel and travel trailer owners
- RV Overnighters Association—for RVers looking to stay overnight at mall and shopping center parking lots for $5 per night

Good Sam, FMCA, and the Escapees RV Club are very well known and their loyal members are very satisfied with their services. We recommend that you evaluate all the user groups based on your needs and that you choose the ones that seem to most closely match the services and products you want. The services and discounts they offer make RVing easier, more fun, and more economical. Because annual dues are very reasonable, many RVers belong to more than one group.

The RV Overnighters Association is a relatively new organization that was created in 2000 in response to the outlawing of overnight RV parking by many communities. This group provides a list of mall, shopping center, and superstore parking lots that allow overnight parking when reservations are made in advance for $5 per night. Annual dues are $30.

RV User Groups with Restricted Membership

A partial list of groups open only to specific people includes:

- Special Military-Active-Retired Travel Club (S.M.A.R.T.)—for active and retired military personnel and their families
- Loners of America—an RV travel club for widows, widowers, divorced people, and those single by choice
- Loners on Wheels—for single men and women
- National Camping Travelers—a Masonic family camping club
- RVing Women—for independent women RVers

RV Manufacturer User Groups

Most of the major RV manufacturers, including Bounder, Winnebago, and Airstream, have created or sponsored organizations whose members are owners of the specific manufacturer's rigs. They provide services and offer discounts on parts, supplies, and branded items, such as T-shirts, coffee mugs, and other souvenirs. The manufacturers also offer to arrange for factory tours. Membership is normally open to any RVer owning a new or used RV, and often the manufacturer will provide a free one-year membership with the purchase of a new RV.

A short list of manufacturers providing and supporting user groups includes Airstream, Allegro, Alpenlite, Avion, Bounder, Discovery, Gulfstream, and Winnebago.

The Bottom Line on User Groups

RVers should not rule out the advantages and opportunities of the many user groups available, but will probably feel better if they discuss any particular group in advance with friends and other RVers. Our book provides only a partial list of the user groups that are available. New and experienced RVers will have fun checking out the information about groups in RV magazines and publications. Those who use the internet can also surf the websites listed in this chapter.

We recommend that you review all the available user groups. Many RVers find that belonging to more than one is worthwhile because each group has its advantages, and some may be unique and of particular interest.

Private Campground Memberships

Coast to Coast Resorts is one example of an RV user group that is open to RVers who own memberships in participating resorts and campgrounds. Coast to Coast Resorts represents approximately 1,000 private campgrounds. Membership benefits include the ability to visit and use facilities at member resorts, discounts at approximately 600 public campgrounds, and a member magazine. Coast to Coast Resorts also provides other RVer-related services, including emergency road service, extended RV warranties, health, home, and auto insurance, and car rental discounts.

There are two ways to establish a permanent home campground or resort. You can choose to purchase your own site or you can purchase a membership at a resort or campground, such as a Coast to Coast member resort, where sites are made available for member stays.

Resorts that sell sites generally provide high-end luxury accommodations with amenities that may include golf, boating, nature trails, a large clubhouse, and extensive exercise and recreational facilities. Purchased sites may cost anywhere from $10,000 to $15,000 and can go up into six figures. RVer-owned sites are frequently roomy and have concrete pads and full utilities. The resort generally allows the owner the opportunity to build various types of structures that may include RV garages, screen rooms, storage buildings, and park models. If you purchase a permanent site, you may want to take some factors and expenses into consideration and at least have these questions answered before signing on the dotted line:

— What is the initial purchase cost?
— Are the maintenance expenses charged quarterly or annually?
— What are the amount and deductibility of local property taxes?
— What are the requirements for insurance?
— Can you rent out the site yourself when you're not using it?
— Can the resort manager rent out the site when you're not using it?
— Can you sell the site or return it to the developer?

- Will you use it enough to justify tying up your investment?
- Does owning the site give you discounts at other participating campgrounds?

RVers considering campground and resort memberships, which usually start at $3,000 and go up, should also consider several important factors and get the answers to some questions. These may include:

- What is the initial cost?
- What is the duration of the membership period? (Memberships may run for extended time periods such as twenty years, thirty years, or lifetime).
- How many days can you stay at a time?
- What are the number of sites available and memberships sold?
- What are the quarterly or annual dues and is there any limit on increases?
- Can you cancel your membership and stop making maintenance payments at any time?
- Can you sell your membership?
- Will you use it enough to justify tying up your investment?
- Does membership give you discounts or reduced rates at other participating campgrounds, such as the Coast to Coast Resorts group?

Another factor for your consideration is that member-owned and membership campgrounds frequently rent a limited number of sites to the public, so you can enjoy the generally excellent services and amenities without having to buy a membership or site.

We recommend previewing and staying at any campground several times before making the decision to buy or join. Many member-owned and membership campgrounds and resorts offer attractive promotions that even include free stays of one or more nights for RVers who want to preview their offerings.

You should consider the purchase of a campground membership or site purchase a long-term legal commitment. Be aware that you can incur considerable expenses or losses by ending a membership or selling an owned site. It also generally takes an extended period of time to revoke, sell, or transfer your member or owner rights.

Discount Cards

RVers can obtain discount cards for many types of services, including fuel, parts and service, and campground fees. Many discount cards are provided free of charge, and most of the others have very low fees that are quickly recouped on your first trip or use. For instance, Passport America is a camping club that provides half off the campground fee at more than 700 campgrounds and RV resorts in the United States, Canada, and Mexico. Passport America can pay for itself with only one trip because the annual membership fee is only $44.

Another discount club for RVers is President's Club, which is issued by Camping World, a major RV equipment, parts, and service provider with approximately thirty locations across the country (see next section). President's Club provides a 10 percent discount on all purchases made at Camping World. Membership also entitles the RVer to periodic newsletters and flyers for special promotions. At a cost of $20 per year, this card generally pays for itself on the first use.

The Flying J R.V. RealValue Club card offers discounts on fuel, propane, food, and services at the nationwide chain of Flying J travel centers. The Flying J locations are very RV-friendly and popular with all RVers. We find the separate, wide RV gas-pump lanes and propane availability to be a real boon because we tow a car. Flying J truck stops give RVers their own separate pumps and provide plenty of room to get in and out. We love that we can get from Florida into southern New Jersey before we run out of Flying Js.

Kampgrounds of America offers its KOA Value Kard for $10 per year. It provides a 10 percent discount on all stays, a free *KOA Directory and Road Atlas*, discount coupons at Prime Outlets malls, a 15 percent discount on Budget car rentals, and a free issue of *Camping Life* magazine. You will also receive notices of special offers and discounts not available to non-cardholders. You can purchase the card when you check into any KOA or you can order it off their website.

The Yogi Bear's Jellystone Park Camp-Resorts offer a program similar to KOA's that provides discounts for all stays. Both the KOA Value Kard and the Yogi Bear's Jellystone Park Camp-Resorts discount cards can be purchased at check-in and used for the first and subsequent stays.

Most of the RV user groups, for example Good Sam, provide membership cards that can be used for discounts (usually 10 percent) at selected campgrounds. They may also provide discounts for other related RV activities, including parts and service and liquid propane (LP) gas suppliers. It's a good idea to verify the campground participation in the discount program when you make your campground reservations and again at check-in. This is necessary because some of the campgrounds and resorts may have changed their affiliation with the discount program since you made your initial reservation. You may also want to tell RV service providers that you are eligible for discounts on parts, service, or LP gas before a work order is written up or before work is started.

For bargain prices on gas, check out buying clubs such as Sam's Club, Price Club, and Costco. Many of the locations sell gas at the lowest possible regional prices and are very helpful when you are not near the interstate or large travel stops. In addition to gas, they also sell tires up to load range E at very competitive prices. We always print out the Sam's Club locations along our route before we hit the road.

Equipment, Parts, Service, and Supplies

RV equipment, parts, service, and supplies are available from a large number of outlets, including:

- Independent RV equipment, parts, and service suppliers
- Total RV service organizations
- RV dealers
- Superstores, big-box stores, and discount stores

Independent RV equipment and parts suppliers generally provide installation and service for any RV equipment sold. Many also provide factory-authorized warranty service and extended warranty service for selected equipment, systems, and accessories.

Total RV service organizations (such as Camping World) sell equipment, parts, supplies, and installation services. They also provide extended warranties on equipment purchased and installed and may also provide catalog services for their products and other related RV services, which can include extended RV warranty contracts, RV loans, RV insurance, discount telephone cards, and banking and credit cards.

RV dealers sell new and used RVs and are service providers. They honor the warranties on RVs sold by RV manufacturers that they represent. RV dealers also provide installation and service for RV equipment and extend discounts for parts, equipment, and service to RVers who buy new or used RVs from the dealership. RV World, the local Winnebago dealer in Nokomis, Florida, who sold us our RV, is a good example and taught us that buying locally is a good deal. RV World gives us a ten percent discount on all our service, repairs, and parts.

RV dealers also are happy to assist their customers and visiting RVers in obtaining problem resolution from the manufacturer when necessary. They usually have large parts inventories and can also expedite delivery of parts from the factory when required and provide RV body shop service and repairs. We had a broken windshield wiper drive assembly on our first long RV trip in our brand-new Winnebago. Upon arriving for our three-night, two-day layover in the Cherry Hill campground in College Park, Maryland, the Winnebago dealer in College Park, Maryland, offered to send employees directly to the campground to make the necessary repairs. They said their location was in a very crowded business area that was difficult to get in and out of, especially with a toad (a towed vehicle). Now that's dealer service!

Many of the RV dealers and independent shops also provide catalog and ordering services for shipment of RV parts and accessories to you at home or on the road.

RVers requiring parts and supplies will be happy to know that many large discount stores, including superstores Kmart and Wal-Mart, carry a limited selection of RV and camping supplies. These can include lightweight folding chairs, lanterns, flashlights, batteries, water hoses, chemicals, sewer hoses, and hookup fittings at very reasonable prices. In areas where boating is popular, such as Florida, the discount superstores may carry 12- and 13-inch trailer tires and complete wheel assemblies at lower prices than tire dealers and RV shops. And don't forget those snacks, books for leisure reading, and sundries!

The luck of the RVer was with us when we blew out a 13-inch car dolly tire on I-75 west of Fort Lauderdale while on a trip to the Florida Keys. After putting on the spare, we kept our eyes peeled and spied a Wal-Mart in Homestead, Florida, on the way to our destination. The Wal-Mart staff were so nice as to replace the defective tire and put it back on the car dolly while we had lunch. It was another great RVing experience that reinforced faith in our fellow humans!

Interstate Exit Guides and Truck Stop Guides

Interstate exit guides can be a godsend for the information they provide about services and businesses located at every exit of the U.S. Interstate Highway System as well as the Trans-Canada Highway. Interstate guides also identify travel centers and fuel stops that have adequate maneuvering space for large RVs and trucks in red boldface type. Examples of facilities highlighted include rest stops, weigh stations, restaurants, travel centers, fuel stops, truck washes, service facilities, and motels. The interstate guides also clearly identify medical facilities near the exits.

The truck stop guides usually list only truck stops and related facilities. Types of information provided include repair facilities, truck washes, and associated restaurant and rest facilities. The advantages of the truck stop guides include their coverage of primary U.S. highways and state roads that handle heavy traffic.

Just because you go roaring down the road with your own kitchen and bathroom doesn't mean that you don't have to find a Dairy Queen or a Cracker Barrel restaurant. (Doesn't everyone need a pineapple shake from Dairy Queen or crave a B.L.T. from Cracker Barrel once in a while?) When desperate for these treats or any other, you can find them if you have on hand such publications as *eXitSource 2001* (formerly *The Exit Authority*) and *eXitSource 2001 RV Directory* (formerly *Travel Centers and Truckstops*). They are both published by eXitSource (previously known as Interstate

America Publications). The name changes became effective in 2001. The books are readily available in bookstores, RV stores, and on the internet. They also provide a website known as eXitSource.com that provides limited information about facilities and services at each exit.

The *Rest Area Guide*, written by Bill Cima and published by Cottage Publications, lists the rest areas and dump stations on the interstate highways, U.S. highways, and state highways, plus other RV information. We find the *Rest Area Guide* helpful for its listing of rest stops on state parkway and turnpike systems that are not in *Exit Authority*, which only lists resources that are located near the exits on the U.S. Interstate Highway System.

Mountain Directories

Owning and reading mountain directories before and during RV trips will help you avoid being caught unawares of steep grades you may have to navigate. Mountain directories tell you how long and steep grades are, the number of lanes on the grade, escape ramps available, switchbacks, and so on.

A mountain guide tells you in advance what you will encounter, so you can, for instance, avoid roaring over a hilltop into a steep, possibly dangerous downgrade or dawdling at the base of a long, steep upgrade. The RVer who avoids exposing the RV to excessive speed and braking problems on downgrades (which can be sheer terror) and avoids overheating the engine and transmission on long upgrades is a happy and safe RVer. RVers who drive gas-powered motorhomes and tow cars or boats (and those who towing travel and fifth-wheel trailers) especially benefit from knowing in advance the locations of steep grades.

Reading a mountain guide while planning your RV trip also gives you the chance to choose an alternative route if you are reluctant to drive in the mountains or hills. On the flip side, you can also choose hilly and mountainous areas simply because you prefer them.

Richard Miller has written two versions of his mountain directory: *Mountain Directory East for Truckers, RV, and Motorhome Drivers* and *Mountain Directory West for Truckers, RV, and Motorhome Drivers*. As "East Coast RVers," we find the eastern version helpful in driving through northern

Georgia, the western Carolinas and Virginia, Pennsylvania, New York, and New England. We'll use the western version when we go cross-country.

RV Website Addresses and Information Links

Expansion in the number of RVers and organizations providing services is reflected in the number of websites providing valuable information.

We recommend "visits" to the sites discussed in this section so you can select the ones you like and that seem to meet your needs. The websites are conveniently grouped below according to different categories. This list is by no means comprehensive, but it is a good start. RVers will benefit from looking at and perusing a multitude of attractive and useful sites. Many sites link to other RV websites. Internet search engines such as Metacrawler (www.metacrawler.com) or Yahoo (www.yahoo.com) are also useful for looking up RV information not available in sites already visited. As with any other internet search, you can stay on-line for hours just by linking from one site to another.

For faster access to the sites you like and find useful, you can bookmark or add websites to your list of Favorites (usually by clicking on the "Favorites" button on your toolbar and then clicking on the "Add to Favorites" button). Both the popular Microsoft Internet Explorer and Netscape browsers as well as the major internet service providers such as AOL and CompuServe make it easy to add, remove, and organize websites you want to reach from your Favorites list. Why remember those web addresses yourself when the computer can do it for you?

There are different types of websites of value to RVers that may be categorized as:

— Corporate websites, such as the Good Sam and FMCA sites, which provide a wide variety of information to their members. These sites provide a combination of information and limited commercial activities or links. Their primary focus is providing information.

— Informational websites, such as the National Park Service, National Highway Traffic Safety Administration, and Military Travel Guide sites, which also provide information but have fewer commercial activities or links.

- Commercial websites, such as the Camping World, Amazon.com, and Campground (KOA and Jellystone) sites, which are designed to help you find specific products you need while also providing information, reservations, and on-line ordering services. Many of these sites provide links to other related sites.

Some websites, such as About.com (which we highly recommend), are a mixture of extensive information and links to services and high-value commercial sites.

User Groups

- www.goodsamclub.com—Good Sam, excellent links to trip routing, construction information, and weather
- www.fmca.com—Family Motor Coach Association, includes information on location of RV dump stations for members
- www.escapees.com—Escapees RV Club, excellent site for full-timers and extended-travel RVers, unique offerings for healthcare, insurance, etc.
- www.fcrv.org—Family Campers and RVers, open to family-oriented members with interests in RVing and tent camping
- www.smartrvclub.org—Special Military-Active-and Retired Travel Club (S.M.A.R.T.), for active and retired military RVers
- www.overnighters.com—RV Overnighters Association, for RVers who want to stay overnight in mall and shopping center parking lots for $5 per night, links to other good RV websites

Campgrounds and Resorts

- www.camping.tl.com—Trailer Life campground and RV information, links to other RV websites
- www.woodalls.com—Woodall's campground and RV information, excellent links to other RV websites
- www.koakampgrounds.com—KOA campgrounds and reservations, trip planner, links to other RV websites

- www.campjellystone.com—Yogi Bear's Jellystone Park Camp-Resorts campgrounds and reservations, links to other RV websites
- www.passportamericacamping.com—Passport America, lists participating campgrounds, links to other websites
- www.gocampingamerica.com—information about 3,500 campgrounds belonging to the National Association of RV Parks and Campgrounds in an easy-to-use and -read format
- www.freecampgrounds.com—index of free and very low-priced campgrounds
- www.rvpark.com—directory listing campgrounds by state, limited information but easy-to-use and -read format
- www.campusa.com—National RV Park Campground Directory and Camping Guide, lists campgrounds by state, limited information but easy-to-use and -read format
- www.bisdirectory.com/camping—Benz's Outdoor Recreation Directory, provides information about campgrounds, weather, tourist information, and extensive links to RV and tourism websites
- www.usastar.com—links to the I-95 Exit Information Guide OnLine, which lists camping areas, RV parks, rest stops, weather, and a mileage calculator for I-95 from Florida to Maine; also links to North American Road Guides for trip planning and mapping, and to extensive travel-related websites and information
- www.nps.gov—National Park Service, provides links to and information about National Parks, including camping, entrance passes, programs, and related items
- www.reserveusa.com—National Recreation Reservation Service, for 1,700 locations managed by the USDA Forest Service and the U.S. Army Corps of Engineers

Miscellaneous Information and Links

- www.camping.about.com—extensive information and links about RV organizations, campgrounds, outdoor activities, suppliers, and related RV activities

- www.rvtravel.about.com—extensive information and links about RV organizations, outdoor activities, RV service and suppliers, and related RV activities
- www.fulltiming-america.com—extensive information and links helpful to all RVers, including dump stations, campgrounds, festivals and events, modem-friendly campgrounds, and insurance
- www.newrver.com—extensive information and links about the buying and financing of RVs, the RV lifestyle, towing, extended warranties, and RV books
- www.rverscorner.com—extensive information and links about maintenance, safety, RVer experiences, campgrounds, etc.
- www.RVersonline.org—extensive information and links for RVers that include technical topics and miscellaneous RV information
- www.usps.com—U.S. Postal Service, provides postal information and trip mapping and routing
- www.campingontheinternet.com—information about using computers plus links to RV websites
- www.quartzsitervshow.com/rvlinks.htm—extensive information about RVs, user groups, jobs, and websites
- www.rv-links.com—a directory of links to a wide variety of useful RV websites
- www.outwestnewspaper.com—helpful "how-to" articles and links to RV websites
- www.amazon.com—large selection of RV books plus other books and media
- www.barnesandnoble.com—large selection of RV books plus other books and media
- www.rvbookstore.com—good for RV books, with links to other book and commercial websites

Supplies, Services, and Maintenance
- www.rv.net—extensive information about maintenance, safety, campgrounds, etc., with links to related websites

- www.campingworld.com—Camping World catalogs and ordering service
- www.flyingj.com—information about the Flying J travel centers and discount cards, locations, and fuel prices
- www.gorp.com—extensive information on outdoor recreation and national parks, with excellent links to other outdoors websites
- www.workamper.com—information about jobs on the road for RVers
- www.nadaguides.com—N.A.D.A. guides for pricing of used cars, RVs, classic cars, marine, aircraft, power sports, and manufactured housing products
- www.nhtsa.dot.gov—National Highway Traffic Safety Administration information regarding all vehicle recalls

Trip Routing and Navigation

- www.delorme.com—click on "EarthaMaps" for mapping service, open to everybody, provides information about DeLorme software mapping products, GPS units, and paper maps and books
- www.goodsamclub.com—trip routing for Good Sam members
- www.mapquest.com—MapQuest trip routing, open to everybody, provides extensive information, access to phone directories, city guides, etc.
- www.mapblast.com—MapBlast trip routing, open to everybody, access to phone directories, downloads to PDAs, etc.
- www.koakampgrounds.com—KOA trip routing, open to everybody, uses MapQuest and allows you to display KOA Kampgrounds along your route
- www.expedia.com—Expedia trip routing, open to everybody, travel information regarding hotels, airlines, etc.
- maps.yahoo.com—Yahoo! maps and trip routing, open to everybody
- www.randmcnally.com—Rand McNally trip routing, open to everybody, uses MapBlast and provides access to their on-line store for all their products
- www.roadguides.com—North American Roadguides trip planning and mapping service, open to everybody, uses MapBlast and has extensive information and links to travel-related websites

TRIP PLANNING THAT WORKS

Effective trip planning gives RVers a comfort level and the assurance that no necessity, or enjoyable and anticipated activity and destination, is overlooked. Of course, each RVer has a different level of tolerance for preplanning. Some of the factors that may determine the amount of necessary advance planning include trip duration, number of stops, and experience. Some RVers only travel with very detailed plans that spell out a structured schedule with reservations to be made as well as locations and sights of interest to be visited. Other RVers prefer a more relaxed and adventurous approach. They are willing to work with a general itinerary that changes based on what happens during the trip.

When embarking on an extended trip, the RVer will probably feel more confident if all the bases are covered in advance, while keeping in mind that things might change along the way. Among others, tasks to be completed before leaving are:

— Prepping the RV for the road
— Arranging for money, banking, and bill paying
— Selecting communication tools to be used on the road
— Handling snail mail (mail delivered by the U.S. Postal Service)
— Securing the home base
— Loading the RV

Chapter 2 deals only with trip planning; the details of the other items on the above list are covered in successive chapters.

One advantage of fully planning your first RV trip is that all subsequent trips will be easier to plan. The learning curve required to be able to quickly set up and execute good trips is far from steep. Therefore, with each subsequent trip, getting out on the road is faster and easier, and the RVer's confidence that all the bases have been covered is greater.

Trip planning questions to consider include:

— What are your destinations?

— Will you be traveling with the support of an RV group?

— How long will each stop be?

— Do you need reservations?

— What trip routing tools will you use?

— Have you planned for RV service on the road?

— What will you need for the Trip Book (see page 39)?

Choosing Your Destinations

Choosing short layover stops on the outbound and return trips may be all that many RVers ever do, but others will want a more structured and planned itinerary.

The latter group chooses the intermediate stopping points based on exploring new areas and routes, enjoying tourist attractions and recreational facilities, and visiting relatives and friends through the complete trip. This tends to make the RV trips a little longer with more time on the road before returning to the home base.

Many RV trips will be adventures that occur on the fly, with traveling planned "by the seat of the pants" for a vacation taken by a family, couple, or group of friends. Traveling with a group is covered further on in this chapter. Having the right tools and information lets you set up a trip very quickly and easily.

One of our most enjoyable trips was an "on the fly" trip to see the Cherry Blossom Festival in Washington, D.C. We were watching a TV news clip about the festival on a Monday evening that said the blossoms would be peaking on the following Sunday. Since we always try to have our RV "ready to roll," we were able to leave Wednesday morning, arrive Friday, and enjoy a spectacular blossoming of the cherry trees around the Washington boat basin. We followed up by stopping in Williamsburg, Virginia, for a couple of days on the way back.

The campground directories and RV-related websites in Chapter 1 (You Can Find the Information You Need, But It May Take a While) provide names, locations, telephone numbers, and area information. We also like to ask other RVers about their experiences, because first-hand accounts are an excellent source of information about campgrounds and resorts, area attractions and services, and roads that they can recommend from first-hand experience.

As RVers, we have our choices of private, public (county, state, and National Park and federal lands), and member only campgrounds and RV resorts. RVers who choose member-only resorts will have to accept the fact that a fair number of member-only resorts make sites available to the public on a space-available basis. The member-only resorts may or may not advertise in the campground directories. Therefore, the savvy RVer will keep on hand copies of the directories provided by private campground organizations, such as "Coast to Coast" that can be helpful in obtaining reservations at private resorts in desired locations. The directories may provide helpful information about resorts and campgrounds not listed, for instance, in Woodall's or Trailer Life directories.

If you are driving a large rig or towing, we strongly recommend using pull-through sites at layover destinations or stops with short stays. As the name implies, a pull-through site allows the RV driver to pull in and pull out of the site without having to back up and maneuver a tight turn. You should know the dimensions of the site before trying to park your RV. Checking in advance or when making reservations is a good idea, because pull-through sites and RV lengths vary. The campground directories provide helpful information regarding campsite size and availability of pull-through sites. *Trailer Life Directory* lists the number and size of pull-through sites at each campground.

Newcomers to the RV community may be most comfortable starting out with trips of shorter duration and mileage. Learning how to handle the RV and its accessories and systems, and setting up and taking down campsites, can take some practice before a satisfactory routine becomes automatic. Short "shakedown" trips are highly recommended after acquiring a new RV, or before setting off on a long trip if the RV has been unused for any length of time.

Excellent information for RV trips in various parts of the United States can be found in *Great RV Trips*, available from Fulcrum Publishing, which details thirteen scenic and interesting trips from Alaska to Florida. Author Charles Cadieux describes many aspects of enjoyable RVing and includes total trip miles and days on the road. Cadieux discusses trips he has taken in an informal and conversational style that makes for a pleasant and informative reading experience. We also use and recommend *Travel Guide—USA*, published by Readers Digest, as an excellent resource for regional maps, tourist attractions, and parks. *Travel Guide—USA*'s compact size and easy-to-read, spiral-bound format make it easy to use.

A Lidstone Law of RVing: When considering campgrounds in areas you'll be visiting for the first time, a consideration of county campgrounds is most advisable. Many county campgrounds, which have very reasonable rates, don't pay for ads in the campground directories. However, our experience has shown that their campsites are large and well maintained. The county campgrounds also often have extensive hiking and recreational facilities.

For more information on visits to national, state, or county parks, see Chapter 4 (Visiting National, State, and County Parks). If you plan to visit Canada or Mexico, take a look at Chapter 5 (Entering Canada and Mexico).

Traveling with the Support of an RV Group

Group travel simply means that two or more RVs get on the road together in a manner that can be more or less structured and organized. Group travel may involve several friends and relatives traveling together on an informal basis to the same destinations. Traveling in groups as a participant in a paid and fully organized RV outing with other RVers is another choice. Such organized trips always have hosts who organize and coordinate activities and collect fees. They may be called rallies, caravans, or (in the case of Good Sam's organized trips) Samborees. The events may last from a few days to a few months and will keep you interested, entertained, and very busy! On organized trips provided by Good Sam and other RVing groups, RVers enjoy entertainment, sightseeing on organized bus tours, planned stops for meals, and informal sightseeing.

The nature of the RV group trip varies, but may include:

- RVers from different locations getting together at a single site or destination
- RVers from different locations getting together at a single starting point for an extended trip with multiple stops and layovers
- Combination trips involving cruise ships, barge trips, or overseas destinations

The largest RV user groups and private commercial organizations sponsor caravans or rallies. The Good Sam Samborees are very popular and well attended. Costs are very reasonable compared to what you would spend traveling alone. The organizers can negotiate discounts not available to individuals for campgrounds and resorts and at area restaurants and attractions because they are bringing in a group.

RVers who sign on for a caravan RV trip organized and coordinated by professionals benefit from the experience of seasoned and expert RVers who know the destination campgrounds, resorts, and local attractions like the backs of their hands. These hosts are experienced guides and "wagon-masters" who ably handle administration details and can assist in obtaining repairs for breakdowns or in resolving other problems that may arise. Participating RVers can relax to a certain extent while enjoying the opportunity to meet new people from all over the United States (or the world) and enjoying the camaraderie of other RVers with similar interests.

Planning Each Stop

The length of time spent at each stop will be determined by a multitude of factors, plans, and considerations that cannot all be listed. However, RVers will benefit from thinking about several considerations. These can include the total time available for the trip; travel time required to get from place to place; desired arrival and departure times; time to be spent with friends and relatives residing in or traveling to the same destinations; and local attractions you want to visit.

However, on extended trips, stops and layovers should be long enough to provide adequate rest and relaxation before resuming driving. We made the mistake of planning too many two- and three-day stopovers on our first long trip and found that setting up and taking down the site began to border on drudgery. We now make sure that most of our destinations that are not one-night stops are given at least four days in length.

Many RVers either dry camp (no hookups) or just hook up electricity for one-night stops when they arrive late and want to leave early and quickly. For new RVers making their initial longer trips, longer stays provide the opportunity to explore the RV and its appurtenances and to learn the best ways to use and enjoy them.

Making Reservations

Whether or not reservations will be waiting at twilight over the next rise or on the horizon depends on the personality and lifestyle of the RVer and on the season or the number of visitors flocking to desired locations. For the free-spirited, having a reservation that confirms the availability of the desired campground or RV resort and requested hookups could take the fun out of RVing. Others may be reluctant to provide credit card numbers over the telephone or the internet. However, other RVers may feel more secure when they have laid out the trip in advance and made reservations they know to be adequate, suitable, and convenient. The last group of RVers like to know that the services and sites they need will be available and waiting when they arrive.

Many campgrounds and resorts give discounts for longer stays. If you're staying several weeks or longer, consider making multiple one-week consecutive reservations and paying up each week. This spreads out your expenses and allows you to shorten a stay more easily if required.

We have found over and over again that campgrounds and RV resorts have reasonable policies that allow for a last-day change of plans on short notice. We have cancelled our reservations while an hour away from the destination on the scheduled day of arrival without any difficulty at all. Campgrounds and RV resorts generally ask for a credit card number when accepting reservations. However, they do not bill you until you show up and use the site. They will charge a one-night fee if you are a no-show and failed to cancel you reservation. The reservation guarantees you a site after a day on the road, and we have never had to pay a cancellation fee.

Some campgrounds and resorts may request a small deposit or one day's rental to secure a reservation. We have found that deposits are generally refunded under most circumstances if you have to cancel. We advise you to always ask for the campground's cancellation policy when making a deposit or providing a credit card number to guarantee a site. It's a good policy to always document reservations, deposits, and cancellation requirements and keep them in the RV Trip Book for quick and accurate reference. The RV Trip Book is discussed later in this chapter.

Several caveats regarding reservations and refunds must be considered. For instance, resort areas may require deposits and longer cancellation notice periods, and may also charge cancellation fees. These requirements are also often enforced during long holiday weekends when campgrounds have more requests for sites than they can fill.

As a considerate RVer, you should always cancel reservations as soon as you know you cannot make a date. This practice not only ensures that you pay no unnecessary no-show or cancellation fees, but also enables the campground to have a site available to another RVer who can make use of it.

Trip Routing Considerations

Trip routing considerations are important. A successful trip is a combination of your personal driving style and needs, the topography and traffic environment of the areas along your route, and the tools and services available to make the overall planning and execution easier.

Route planning and selection are important because they get you to your stopovers and final destination reasonably on schedule. RV information resources that help in selecting a route include campground directories, road atlases, maps, exit and truck stop guides, mountain guides, and computer mapping and routing software.

Your trip routing is based on:

- Roads you prefer to drive
- Intended daily departure and arrival times
- Number of miles you would like to cover
- Availability of stopover campgrounds and resorts
- Average speed
- Weather
- Towing
- Whether driving is being shared

Excellent and free trip routing services are provided at no cost to members of AAA, Good Sam, and the major RV user groups. These organizations can also provide information and suggestions about areas being visited, construction activity, campgrounds and resorts, and state laws affecting RVers. We've provided extensive information to help you with trip routing and other trip planning services in Chapter 12 (How to Keep from Getting Lost).

After selecting your route, we advise that you make a list of the roads, exits, and road changes by exit/mile marker. Having this list handy makes it a lot easier for the copilot to keep an eye out for exits and route changes. An ordered list of the trip's twists, turns, exits, and routes makes it easy to plan stops and to see them coming. A map can also be marked up. These handheld references can help you avoid overshooting your exit or destination at 70 miles an hour when you have only a vague recollection as to what was discussed and agreed upon at breakfast.

Safety Considerations

Because you want to arrive safely while having a good time driving your rig, you must stay alert. This means keeping your daily driving abilities at an optimum level. To do so, you will have to factor in and adjust for delays and bad weather.

You should never try to drive while tired. Coffee does not do it. RVers have the luxury of traveling pretty much as they want to and according to their own schedules and needs. There is no need to ever be tired. Therefore, take that nap in the far reaches of the Wal-Mart parking lot when you need it, even during the day, rather than getting tired. Wal-Mart will not care a whit, as long as you buy a tube of toothpaste (or something that costs even less). If the local sheriff's deputy knocks on the door and wakes you up, explain the situation and offer your friendly police officer a coke or a cup of coffee. You can then explain that you will be on the road within a few hours.

It is far safer to get off the road before your planned stop than to expose yourself, your passengers, and other drivers on the road to possible injury or death.

The trip routing tools will help you easily adjust your trip itinerary due to traffic delays or bad weather.

Scheduling RV Service While on the Road

Making appointments at appropriate service facilities before leaving the home base is a good idea if the mileage or duration of an extended trip will require scheduled maintenance while traveling. Inform the service manager when you can, in advance, that you will be in the area of the particular service facility while traveling and would like to wait while the service is being performed. Also be sure to make contact with the shop several days before the scheduled service date to follow up and reconfirm your time slot and the current availability of all parts and service.

RV service providers are listed by area in the campground directories, interstate exit guides, and truck stop guides discussed in Chapter 1, and RV coach and chassis documents covered in Chapter 16 (Manuals and Other RV Documents).

The All-Important Trip Book

The Trip Book provides an easy "catchall" method to keep track of the miscellaneous odds and ends of trip planning. Barbara likes the Trip Book because she is a tree hugger. Barbara saves all the brochures so they won't be gathered up again on a subsequent trip to the same location. The Trip Book also helps us remember the places we enjoyed so much and provides the information we need to enjoy our time there again. Barbara uses a separate tabbed folder for each state visited, as a start. Of course, we can make as many subfolders as we want! The folders used by Barbara the Tree Hugger represent only a small portion of the paper handouts you would otherwise acquire and discard while RVing. We recommend keeping the Trip Book in a three-ring binder.

Trip Book items we find helpful include:

— Delineation of the travel route with rest stops, fuel stops, and food stops recorded by exit/mile markers

— Trip itinerary listing the dates, mileage, campgrounds/RV resorts, phone numbers, miscellaneous comments, and information regarding deposits, cancellations, and so on

— Copies of campground and RV resort brochures and receipts for deposits

— Area maps of various destinations

— Checklists for loading the RV and setting up and taking down the RV site

— List of debit, ATM, and credit card account numbers, addresses, and phone numbers in case of loss or theft

— Phone numbers for emergency contacts, doctors, pharmacies, medical service providers, and road service

— Copy of RV registration, proof of insurance, and extended warranty

The three-ring binder makes it easy to add new items to the Trip Book or to remove outdated items. Multiple items for the same location can be stored in filing sleeves of various types that can be obtained inexpensively from the office supply superstores.

We use an inexpensive, soft-sided fabric attaché carrying case to hold the RV Trip Book, RV manual and documents, and personal items such as our address book, checkbook, pencils and pens, writing paper, envelopes, and stamps. The cloth attaché is more flexible and is less likely to cause damage than a hard-sided attaché when stowed in any snug area.

Because many RVers visit the same areas, campgrounds, and resorts more than once, keeping travel materials in the Trip Book provides quick access to needed information when planning more visits.

Building the RV Library

As you go through the different chapters of this book, you will be seeing comments and suggestions about a variety of publications that you might want in your personal RV library. Extensive information is readily available about all aspects of RV activity, including the resources mentioned in Chapter 1.

The complete list of resources we utilize is as follows:

— Campground directories

— Exit and truck stop guides

— Mountain directories

— RV parts and equipment catalogs

— RV trips and travel books for different regions

— State and national park guides

— Technical information on RV operations, use, and maintenance

Chapter 16 (Manuals and Other RV Documents) details the four types of technical documents available to RVers that cover the operations, use, and maintenance of the RV coach, chassis and power train, systems and accessories, and generic RV maintenance and repair manuals.

In addition to the excellent magazines and newsletters published by the user groups, Woodall publishes regional newsletters that include resources and maintenance tips worth keeping. We recommend that you review what's available in RV stores such as Camping World, as well as what's available in bookstores and on the internet, and select the materials you like.

You may want to review the contents of your RV library before each trip to decide which books to bring. Obviously, the campground directories and exit guides go on just about every trip. However, only the adventurous RVer traveling in the summer will need, for instance, a book about Branson, Missouri, while traveling I-95 from Florida to Maine.

We find it convenient to keep a recent Camping World catalog and the previous year's phone book in the RV. (Barbara also keeps an outdated JCPenney catalog under the galley sink in the RV for scraping plates before washing them.) Your library, like ours, is likely to expand quickly. You will probably start out with two or three books but will soon need to find room for fifteen or twenty! However, you will doubtless find all the resources in your personal RVing library to be helpful in planning trips; keeping up with

RV products and technology; supplying maintenance tips and guidance; and using and enjoying your RV on every trip.

RVs, Computers, and the Internet

The personal computer, especially in its ability to connect to the internet, can be a big help to you at home and on the road. The many software programs available for personal finance, e-mail, word processing, and trip planning, mapping, and navigation are fun to use and can make your RV trips easy to plan.

How to Get Internet Access

To get connected to the internet you need a modem in your computer to receive and transfer information, a software package from your internet service provider (offered at no extra cost), and access (a physical link) to the internet.

There are several ways to connect your personal computer (PC) to the internet. You can connect using your PC with a:

- Standard modem connected to a telephone line or cellular phone
- Cable modem connected to a cable TV service provider
- High-speed telephone modem connected to a high-speed telephone service provider
- Satellite modem connected via telephone line and satellite dish

Connecting at Home

Connecting by standard modem and telephone line is the cheapest and most straightforward way. You simply use the modem that came installed in your computer at the time of purchase.

You will choose your home connection method based on desired performance (data transmission speed). Cable, high-speed telephone line, and satellite connections have the fastest data transfer rates and the highest costs. High-speed connections generally cost at least $40 per month and may have installation and setup charges. High-speed connections require a specialized modem, which may be available from the service provider or will otherwise have to be purchased separately. The current satellite hookups generally require a phone line and are very expensive.

Cable and high-speed telephone connections are not yet available for RVers or other users traveling in automotive vehicles. However, satellite internet service providers are currently trying to implement internet access that uses a digital TV satellite dish and eliminates the need for a telephone line.

Connecting on the Road

Most RVers on the road access the internet by connecting their computer to a telephone wall jack or cellular phone. Many campgrounds and RV resorts have telephone line access available for RVers at the store, office, or clubhouse.

Campground directories identify RV campgrounds and resorts that are known to be internet-friendly. A limited number include individual telephone lines at all or selected sites. In addition, some of the resorts can arrange for telephone line installations, through the local telephone company, at sites for seasonal visitors.

If you plan to use your cellular phone, we recommend that you purchase a plan with a high number of minutes and free long distance. To give some perspective, 1,000 minutes a month is only 33 minutes a day of phone use.

Campgrounds that provide telephone jacks in the campground store, office, or clubhouse do so for all RVers. Because other guests may be lining up behind you to use the facilities, it's important that you not settle in for too long. If possible, enter your e-mail text into your computer before you log on, upload your outgoing messages, download your incoming messages, and read them after you disconnect from the phone line.

Powering a Computer in an RV

We recommend that you plug your PC into an uninterruptible power supply (UPS) device or use an inverter with adequate power whenever using a computer in an RV. These devices provide "clean" 120-volt (AC) power to prevent damage to your PC during power failures. They also protect against damage from power surges and low voltages, which are sometimes experienced in campgrounds and RV resorts. Power surges and high or low voltages can cause serious and expensive damage to a desktop or laptop PC.

The UPS device plugs into a 120-volt (AC) outlet and contains backup capability from the combination of a built-in battery and an inverter. It uses the campground or resort 120-volt (AC) power to charge the built-in battery and the inverter to convert the battery power to "clean" 120-volt (AC) power. Its size is no larger than a shoe box, and may be considerably smaller. They have a cost of approximately $40–$100 and are readily available from office supply outlets and computer outlets such as Staples, Office Depot, OfficeMax, Circuit City, and Best Buy. The UPS has sufficient battery power to maintain the PC for ten to twenty minutes to allow you to save files and turn the computer off during a power outage.

An inverter is a device that converts 12-volt (DC) power to 120-volt (AC) power. If your RV does not have an inverter, you can purchase a small one for $40–$90 to operate your desktop computer, laptop computer, or other small 120-volt (AC) appliances or accessories. Inverters are readily available from Camping World and other RV supply stores, electronic stores such as Best Buy or Circuit City, and on the internet. Small 140- to 150-watt inverters weigh about 2 pounds and measure about $1^{1}/_{2}$ by 5 inches. The 300-watt inverters weigh about 3 pounds and are slightly larger.

This is how the process works when using an inverter: Your RV's power converter charges the RV and coach 12-volt (DC) batteries during normal availability of a campground's 120-volt (AC) power. Inverters convert the 12-volt (DC) power from the coach batteries back to 120-volt (AC) power for the computer. In the event of power failure, the inverter continues converting the battery power to 120 volts (AC) as long as the battery voltage is 9.5 volts or greater.

We recommend that RVers using laptop or notebook computers consider an inverter rather than a UPS device. Laptops do not need a UPS device to provide safe power because they are powered by the laptop's internal battery, even when plugged into a 120-volt (AC) power source. The use of an inverter also allows you to use your laptop while driving without worrying about battery life (about two hours for most laptops and portables).

Internet Service Providers

Internet services were originally fee-based and developed by CompuServe, AOL, and Prodigy. Gradually, additional fee-based service providers came on-line, and eventually free internet service became available.

Fee-Based Internet Service Providers

Internet access is available from a wide variety of service providers, most of whom charge by the month. You generally have to provide a debit or credit card account number for billing. Well-known service providers include CompuServe, AOL, MSN, Prodigy, EarthLink, Mindspring, AT&T, Sprint, and Verizon. Also, most telephone companies provide internet access and have combination packages of local, long distance, and internet services available to subscribers.

Fee-based internet service providers often provide access from local telephone numbers (throughout the United States and Canada) to their services. They provide long distance access numbers, and charge for connect time by the minute, when local numbers are not available. They also provide free customer service both on-line and via telephone to their subscribers. If you travel a lot, check the availability of local access numbers at your destinations when selecting a provider.

Free Internet Service Providers

If you want to consider using one of the free internet service providers, remember it is a caveat emptor type of environment. The market is very competitive and volatile. As a result, new providers are offering internet access, and existing providers are often changing their offerings or going out of business.

As mentioned above, there are a number of free internet service providers offering connectivity on a nationwide basis in the United States. They provide free access to the internet and free e-mail service in exchange for the right to display advertising banners on your screen while you are connected. A small number might charge a nominal setup fee to open an account or limit connect time. These providers frequently limit the number of hours of free service, and exceeding this limit will result in charges being assessed.

A number of the merchandisers, such as Wal-Mart, Spiegel, and Kmart, offer free internet access and service. The CDs with all the necessary software and account setup information are generally displayed at the checkout counters, or the retailer will mail them to customers as part of a no-cost marketing promotion.

Free internet service providers attempt to provide access from local telephone numbers to their services from anywhere in the United States and Canada. However, you may have to dial in through their backup access numbers and pay for connect time by the minute, or make a long distance call to an access number for connect time when local numbers are not available at your RV destinations.

A sample, and by no means complete, list of free internet and/or e-mail service providers includes:

- Juno—www.juno.com
- Lycos—www.lycos.com (free e-mail only)
- Alta Vista—www.altavista.com (free e-mail only)
- Address.com—www.address.com
- DotNow—www.dotnow.com
- Netzero—www.netzero.com
- BlueLight—www.bluelight.com

If you are using a free internet service provider, we suggest you consider additional or backup providers in the event your current provider does not meet your needs or is no longer available.

You can use your internet search engine and do a keyword search on "free internet providers" to find what is currently available. Review the offerings closely to compare the free and low-cost internet services, because the services may have restrictions, limits on monthly connect time, or require "membership fees."

CHAPTER 3

MAKING THE TRIP COMFORTABLE

Extended-trip RV travel differs greatly from short trips of a few days; extended trips require a little more "logistics" planning. You almost have to think like a ship's chandler, who must provision a ship to set sail. You get one chance to load up, and you would like to get it right before you're under way. Even though services and products will probably be available along the way, it's preferable to just breeze through the trip without unexpected stops that could be less than enjoyable.

When planning an extended trip, you should consider such requirements as:

- Arranging for local transportation at your destination
- Towing options and requirements
- Additional cooler, refrigerator, and freezer capacity
- Entertainment media
- Patio accessories for warm-weather destinations
- Weather information
- Laundry capability and supplies
- Computers
- Medical, dental, and prescription needs
- Cool- and cold-weather RVing

Local Transportation and Towing

Some RVers prefer to visit places where they can walk to all needed services or points of interest. These RVers make their advance plans accordingly, or find out from the locals where to go and how to get there. Some campgrounds and resorts have free or low-cost shuttle and trolley services to nearby towns and shopping and sightseeing areas.

Many RVers bring bikes with them or are able to rent bikes at their destinations. Some bring scooters, mopeds, or motorcycles, and some make arrangements to borrow a car from friends or relatives or rent a car at their various destinations. Bicycle racks, moped racks, and motorcycle racks are available from RV suppliers. The moped and motorcycle racks are usually mounted on the tow-hitch receiver. Consider purchasing protective covers if you are carrying these types of personal transportation.

If you opt to rent a car, the biggest problem is arranging for pickup and return of the car. Consider using a rental car agency that provides free pickup and delivery service for the person renting the car while staying at a campground or resort. Enterprise Rent-a-Car will pick you up at the campground, take you to the rental office to complete the necessary paperwork, and give you the car. They will also "deliver" you back to the campground or resort when you return the rental car.

However, most RVers who drive motorhomes prefer and enjoy the convenience and flexibility of having their own cars while traveling. These RVers fit their rig with the necessary hardware that allows a car to be towed behind the RV. Most RVers elect to tow a vehicle using a tow bar, a tow dolly, or an auto trailer. The choice is a personal decision, although there are advantages and disadvantages for each, as explained in the following paragraphs.

A Lidstone Law of RVing: It is very dangerous to back up a motorhome while towing a vehicle! Unlike two-wheel trailers, a toad will begin to lift on one side and may tip over unless it is backed up in a straight line. Although you may be able to back up 5–10 feet, anything past that starts the toad turning and lifting on one side with generally disastrous results.

Determining Your Tow Capability

RVers electing to tow a vehicle or trailer should verify that the RV tow-hitch receiver, drawbar, and ball are adequate for the weight of their tow bar, dolly, or auto trailer, and loaded toad. The tow-hitch receivers on most gas-powered motorhomes are rated at 3,500 pounds or 5,000 pounds. To tow safely, the drawbar and ball capacity ratings must be at least as high as the hitch receiver's rating. Hitches are available for more than 5,000 pounds if the chassis is rated for the increased load, and diesel motorhomes may be available with Class IV hitch receivers up to a 10,000-pound capacity. If your tow bar or car dolly plus loaded vehicle weight is close to or exceeds the hitch rating, you will need a higher-capacity hitch. The price difference to upgrade the hitch-receiver capacity is reasonable if installed at the factory.

In addition to the tow-hitch receiver, drawbar, and ball capacity, it is important that you do not exceed the combined gross weight rating (CGWR) of your RV. The CGWR is the combined weight of the RV, tow bar or dolly, and towed vehicle. Exceeding the CGWR will overstress the engine, transmission, chassis, and braking system of your motorhome. The only solutions are to get a bigger RV with a higher CGWR or to get a lighter toad.

If you are purchasing a motorhome, verify that the hitch-receiver capacity and the CGWR are adequate for your needs. Exceeding the tow capability of your RV is very dangerous and exposes you and other vehicles on the road to major injury and damage.

Tow Bars

The advantages of tow bars include their easy hookup, excellent towing performance, and minimal maintenance. Hookup or disconnect time is generally less than five minutes.

However, installing a tow bar requires some rewiring of the auto to be towed. Most tow vehicles require a wiring assembly for lighting, tow-bar attachment fittings, a transmission disconnect feature, and a brake package. Choose your toad carefully, because if you later replace the toad, you will have to install all these components on the replacement vehicle.

A very limited number of front-wheel-drive vehicles can be towed without a transmission disconnect feature. If you are purchasing a vehicle to be towed, ask for a copy of the manufacturer recommendations for towing in writing (do not accept the verbal statements of sales personnel). You will be safer if you install a brake package on the tow vehicle, especially if the vehicle is heavy or the weight exceeds various state limits. Many braking systems are available for installation on toads.

The cost of a tow-bar system varies and is determined by which components are selected (tow bar, mounting system, transmission disconnect, braking system, and miscellaneous accessories, fittings, and adapters). The price ranges are approximately $300–$750 for the tow bar, $150–$350 for the mounting system, $500–$1,000 for the transmission disconnect, $700–$1,000 for the braking system, plus related installation costs.

Although inexpensive A-frame tow bars are available for occasional use, they are not recommended for RVers who tow on a regular basis. Hooking up is more difficult and time consuming than the better "one-person" models designed for motorhome use.

Again, it is important that you don't exceed your CGWR for towing and that your tow-hitch receiver and all of the components of your tow-bar system have load-capacity ratings higher than the combined weight of the tow-bar system and toad.

Tow bars with their required vehicle-equipment modifications and additions are the most popular method of towing a vehicle. They are popular because after the initial installation and refitting of the toad, the RVer can hitch up and get on the road quickly. Tow bars also give the rig and toad a more unified and slicker look than that of the RV–toad–tow dolly package.

Tow Dollies

The primary advantage of tow dollies is the elimination of any need to modify the tow vehicle. You need to be aware of the following requirements for using a tow dolly:

— Tow dollies should only be used for front-wheel-drive vehicles.
— The weight of your tow vehicle should not exceed the load capacity of the tow dolly.
— The combined weight of the loaded tow vehicle and tow dolly should not exceed the hitch capacity and CGWR capacity of your RV.
— The tow dolly requires both a braking system and a breakaway system if the combined weight of the loaded tow vehicle and tow dolly exceeds the pertinent state regulations regarding towing or the weight limits established by the RV manufacturer.

Tow dollies cost approximately $1,000–$2,000, and most tow dollies do not have a braking system. Tow dolly braking systems (surge or electric) are available as an optional feature on selected tow dollies. There are also "add-on" kits to upgrade selected tow dollies. The cost of either braking solution increases the cost of the tow dolly by approximately $600–$800.

Disadvantages of tow dollies include the need to maintain the tow dolly (lubricate wheel bearings and miscellaneous fittings, monitor tires, check the straps regularly for wear and tightness, etc.); lack of braking systems on most tow dollies; length of time and effort required to hitch up the tow dolly and to drive the car on and off the dolly; and the need to connect and disconnect straps each time the car is towed. When considering purchase and use of a tow dolly, you should contact the state Motor Vehicle Bureau to determine if your tow dolly requires license plates and liability insurance.

As with all light trailers, a tow dolly's wheel bearings should be repacked every 10,000 miles or as specified by the manufacturer. It is important to check the straps for wear every time you use the dolly. Replacement straps are available from Camping World and RV parts suppliers.

If your dolly requires a wrench for the straps, we recommend you carry a spare wrench or appropriate-size socket in your toolbox. Otherwise, if you lose your wrench on the road with the toad on the dolly (say that three times quickly!), you might have to cut the restraining straps to release the toad if you can't borrow or buy a replacement wrench.

Auto Trailers

The auto trailer has a dual axle. The toad is driven up onto the bed of the trailer and secured; most have brakes and a flatbed. The advantage of an auto trailer is that the towed vehicle is completely off the ground, which eliminates tire wear and stress on the steering and suspension systems. Auto trailers are available in flatbed or full-enclosure configurations to provide maximum protection for the toad. You can tow any vehicle that does not exceed the trailer's capacity.

The disadvantages of auto trailers are their cost and weight. Weight is usually at least 1,000–1,500 pounds. Auto trailers are only appropriate for towing behind larger motorhomes that have the engine power to handle the total weight of the RV, toad, and auto trailer. Also, as with all light trailers, periodic maintenance is required to repack wheel bearings and to check, adjust, service, and maintain the brake and lighting systems.

As with tow bars and tow dollies, you must make sure that all components of your tow-hitch receiver, draw bar, and ball are adequate for the combined weight of the auto trailer and vehicle; that the weight of the vehicle does not exceed the trailer's carrying capacity; and that you comply with the RV manufacturer's gross vehicle weight rating (GVWR) and combined gross weight rating (CGWR) limits.

Spare Tires and Rims

We recommend that all RVers carry spare tires (mounted on rims) inflated to the correct air pressure for the RV, car dolly (if using one), and toad. We also recommend that you carry emergency road service to change flat tires or blowouts because of the size and weight of RV tires (especially Load Range G), need for heavy-duty wrenches and jacks, and possible need for towing.

Almost all Class C motorhomes, gas-powered Class A motorhomes, travel trailers, and fifth-wheel trailers come with a spare tire and storage or mounting space. Unfortunately, many of the rear-engine diesel motorhomes include neither a spare tire and wheel assembly nor adequate storage space, which are forfeited because of the large size and weight of the tires (frequently on 22.5-inch rims), the lack of available space at the rear end of the chassis for tire storage, and the need to utilize the storage bays for housing other equipment.

Carrying a spare is an individual decision, and we feel you should strongly review your options. We realize that proper tire service and maintenance and attention to weight distribution reduces the odds of having a flat tire or blowout, and that many RVers have never had any tire problems.

The advantages of having a spare tire include:
— Minimizing the amount of time lost off the road
— Limiting the amount of time the RV is in a potentially risky location (busy interstate or highway, narrow road, poorly lighted area, etc.)

— Being able to change the flat yourself if emergency road service is unavailable

— Avoiding the need for towing the RV

You should carry reflective safety triangles, flashlights, lug wrench, jack, and air compressor whether or not you have emergency road service coverage. You will need the jack and lug wrench and air compressor if emergency road service is unavailable and you change the tire yourself, or if the service personnel do not bring a large-enough jack to lift your RV.

If you elect not to carry a "ready-to-roll" spare tire to save weight and storage space or because the RV has no spare tire storage space, you have some additional factors to consider:

— You will need appropriate emergency road service insurance.

— You will need to carry a cellular phone to call for assistance.

— If the toad or tow dolly has the flat and no spare is available, you can drive the RV if you unhook the toad or tow dolly and leave it behind.

— If the RV has the flat and no spare is available, you can unhook the toad and drive it while leaving the RV behind.

— You will require tow service to move the RV (other than a very short distance) if you lose a front RV tire. If you have to move the RV and have the necessary equipment but no road service is available, then one possible option is to remove one of the rear tires and mount it on the front and follow the suggestion in the next bullet.

— You may be able to drive the RV slowly, carefully, and with emergency flashers on if you lose a rear tire mounted on a dual axle and there is no other damage caused as a result of the flat tire or blowout.

— The emergency road service personnel will have to bring out a tire, dismount the wheel with the flat tire, break it down, mount the new tire on the existing rim, and remount the wheel assembly.

— If the rim is damaged, the emergency road service personnel will have to locate and bring out a replacement rim.

— You may have to pay higher prices than necessary for tires or rims because there is no opportunity to comparison shop.

- Specific brand or unique tire requirements, such as low-profile tires, or the need for replacement rims, can result in delays of as many as several days.
- You will increase your expenses and time lost off the road if you must rely on emergency road service to remove a flat and provide you with a spare.

I Want My Big Refrigerator!

The standard refrigerator in most RVs has 8 cubic feet of storage if a two-door refrigerator/freezer, and 10 cubic feet of storage if a side-by-side refrigerator/freezer version. This standard size is adequate for short trips, but RVers always seem to be running out of refrigerator space on longer trips or when traveling with more than two people.

We looked into all the options for obtaining more refrigerator/freezer space on the road or in the campground and chose one of the cheapest: the portable 12-volt (DC) electric cooler. We have found it to be an excellent choice that fits in well on all trips. When we are not driving, the cooler is at the front of our RV between two chairs or in front of the couch. We put an attractive, small rag rug on top and use it as a coffee table. When we drive, the cooler has a place of honor on the couch, plugged into the dashboard, and keeps our cold drinks and fresh fruit handy. However, several other options are also available.

Here are the choices for extra refrigerator (and sometimes freezer) space:
- Twelve-volt (DC) cooler/warmers that plug into a 12-volt (DC) power source (e.g., cigarette lighter) like ours (which we purchased refurbished for $60), are available in a variety of sizes from about 1.0 to 2.5 cubic feet with a cooling or heating capability of approximately 40 degrees below or above the RV's interior temperature. The cost range is $60–$150. The advantages of these are low price and the fact that an inverter or 120-volt (AC) power is not required. Note that 120-volt (AC) power-pack adapters and battery savers are available at an extra charge of approximately $25–$50.
- Compact 120-volt (AC) refrigerator/freezers with 1.7 to 4.3 cubic feet of space are recommended for RVs with inverters and adequate battery power. It is important to purchase the most electrically efficient model to

minimize battery drain (when using an inverter) on the road, and to measure the outside refrigerator dimensions for installation fit, ease of installation and removal, and airflow. A variety of models are available at a cost of $70–$100 for the 1.7- and 2.5-cubic-foot models, and at a cost of $120 for the 3.5- and 4.3-cubic-foot models. They are readily available at all appliance stores and superstores (e.g., Kmart, Wal-Mart, etc.).

— Refrigerator/freezers that plug into a 12-volt (DC) or 120-volt (AC) power source are available from Norcold in a variety of sizes from about 1.5 to 2.0 cubic feet and have both cooler and freezer capability. They have a cooling capability of approximately 80 degrees below the RV's interior temperature and are expensive, with a cost range of $750–$1,100.

— The portable three-way refrigerator from Dometic runs on 12 volts (DC), 120 volts (AC), or propane, and can be purchased at a cost of approximately $400. The unit has about 1.5 cubic feet of storage and snap-on wheels for maneuverability.

— Stand-alone ice makers can free up freezer space. They cost approximately $700–$800 plus installation.

Entertainment Media

RVers who will be away from home for more than a week or two may want to consider bringing along extra onboard entertainment options. We enjoy using our VCR, additional TV, satellite dish and receiver, and enhanced stereo and CD systems. Other items that people may miss while traveling (but that can be taken along by RVers!) include DVD players, tape players, and computers.

What? Another TV?

Although most RVs have one permanently installed TV, many RVers would like an additional TV for the bedroom or outside use with a 9-inch, 12-inch, or 13-inch screen. Small color TVs running on 120 volts (AC) cost approximately $80–$100. They are now available with built-in AM/FM radios or VCRs for approximately $15–$25 more. If you are buying a new TV, be sure to measure the space where you intend to put it in the RV, especially the height of the area. Check the actual fit before you discard the packing materials. If it doesn't fit, return it for a set with smaller dimensions.

Another, slightly more expensive alternative for the small TV is one that runs on 12 volts (DC) or 120 volts (AC) and costs approximately $150 and up. The RVer must determine if this 12-volt (DC) feature is worth the price. If you anticipate using a TV without 120 volts (AC), such as during dry camping or in rest stops, you may want this capability. We purchased a 9-inch color TV with a built-in VCR player/recorder that came with a 120-volt (AC) power cord and 12-volt (DC) power cord from SAM'S Club for $150. The other option for watching TV without 120-volt (AC) power is to use a small inverter to power an inexpensive 120-volt (AC)—only TV (most small color TVs only need 65–100 watts of power).

Dishing Up TV

The best way not to miss your TV shows is to bring them with you. Satellite dishes and receivers guarantee consistent access to TV channels as long as weather permits. They may not work in heavy rain.

The two main satellite TV transmission service providers are DIRECTV and DISH Network, and they have similar pricing and offerings. Their coverages are very similar to those of cable companies. The major networks (ABC, CBS, NBC, and FOX) are now available via satellite. The only difference for satellite coverage on the road, versus at home, is that you cannot get pay-movies unless you can establish a telephone hookup at the site.

A complete satellite system includes the satellite dish and a receiver. Satellite receivers have proprietary technology depending on the service provider, so pick your provider before you buy a receiver. The receivers are priced at $80–$500. Various models are priced differently based on the features provided, which can include the ability to receive multiple channels, freeze-frame capability, time-delay and advanced video services, and e-mail access.

Winegard is the primary manufacturer of low-end and mid-range satellite dishes. Winegard's products span the gamut from stand-alone dishes to manually adjusting roof-mounted dishes to fully automatic roof-mounted dishes, with a price range of approximately $100–$1000. Installation is always extra. Winegard dish products must be raised only while parked at the RV site and cannot be used while driving. If you have a manual crank-up Winegard dish, an elevation indicator box, which costs about $80 plus installation, will considerably speed and ease setup. You will need a compass if you have a manual satellite dish.

RVers also have the opportunity to obtain KVH TracVision dish antennas that are roof-mounted and covered with a dome. These automatically acquire the satellite signals. They are available in models that can operate while the RV is in motion (approximately $2,200–$3,000 plus installation) and in models that can only be used while parked (approximately $1,400 plus installation). The look of the antenna is more aesthetically pleasing than the look of the other options, and the antenna is also protected from the weather, especially rain and snow.

RVers have their choice of DIRECTV or the DISH Network for satellite service. Both providers periodically have special offers for reduced charges for antennas, receivers, and program offerings that may require a minimum sign-up period.

Neither provider charges an initial activation fee and both allow you to turn the service on and off. Before selecting a provider, we recommend you contact the providers to verify the current fees for:

— Activation fee to start service

— Monthly service fee

— Turning service on or off

— "Suspended" status availability and fees

— Cancellation fee to end all service

DIRECTV allows you to turn service off at no cost and charges a $25 fee to reactivate your service. No charges are incurred while satellite service is turned off. There is no fee to cancel service permanently as long as any minimum sign-up period conditions have been satisfied.

RVers using DISH TV have two options for turning service off. They can transfer to "suspend" status, which costs $5.00 per month with no reactivation fee; or cancel service at no cost and pay a $25 fee to reactivate service. As with DIRECTV, there is no fee to cancel service permanently as long as any minimum sign-up period conditions have been satisfied.

In summary, the RVer's options for the satellite dish include:

- Manually adjusting Winegard dish on stand outside of RV (approximately $100–$190)
- Manual crank-up Winegard dish and Winegard Digital Magic elevation indicator box (approximately $240 plus installation)
- Winegard automatic dish and satellite locator (approximately $900 plus installation)
- KVH TracVision low-profile dish under dome with automatic satellite locator while parked (approximately $1,400 plus installation)
- KVH TracVision low-profile dish under dome with automatic satellite locator while parked or driving (approximately $2,200–$3,000 plus installation)—requires use of generator or inverter while driving

One advantage of the manual satellite dish on a remote stand is the ability to move the dish if tree limbs block the antenna's signal. An installed, permanently mounted satellite antenna on the RV may be more convenient and less expensive than the manual satellite dish and remote stand.

We use the manual crank-up Winegard dish with the Winegard Digital Magic elevation box and generally complete the setup within five to ten minutes.

External/Additional Entertainment Center

Many RVs have a permanently installed external entertainment unit with a CD and/or tape player, radio, TV antenna outlet, and 120-volt (AC) and 12-volt (DC) outlets accessible from the outside of the RV. They are usually located in an accessible storage bay or separate compartment under the patio awning, and many include a convenient slideout table. In addition, many RVers bring along a compact high-quality Sony or Bose radio/CD player for use inside the RV.

Privacy and Climate Control

Longer trips generally mean staying in campgrounds and resorts for longer periods. Because the RV already has a large awning, RVers should consider carrying a sunscreen and a screen room.

The sunscreens are lightweight, store compactly, can be attached in about two minutes, and do an excellent job of blocking the rays of the sun while admitting light. Screen rooms are very helpful on those occasions when bugs and mosquitoes present a problem. They also provide a feeling of privacy and a "porch" feeling rather than a "patio" feeling. They generally weigh 35–45 pounds and take about twenty minutes to put up and take down.

Weathering the Storm

Be sure to lower one end of the awning and use awning anchors or tie-downs if you leave your RV for more than a few minutes. We recommend raising your awnings before bad weather hits. Most awnings, if not lowered at one end, will collect water in the center during heavy rain of any significant duration. In addition, if it's windy, the combination of the weight of the trapped water and the force of the wind creates stress that may result in extensive damage. The awning may tear, or the awning track or side braces can rip out of the RV sidewall.

We saw these events (excessive water pooling and high wind) happen in Charleston, South Carolina, during a spring storm that whipped up quickly and unexpectedly while RV owners were sightseeing. Going outside after the storm ended, we found that two RVs within eyeshot had lost their awnings. Luckily, a repairman came out the next day and replaced both awnings! (We didn't ask how much the repairs cost, but we sure did wonder.)

Automated Notification of
Bad Weather and Dangerous Conditions

Adverse weather conditions, including high winds, thunderstorms, tornadoes, heavy rains, and flash floods always present very dangerous situations to RVers and their RVs on the road or in campgrounds or resorts. An RV traveling on the road is not a safe place to be in any type of severe weather. An RV can also be dangerous in very high winds while parked. However, RVers can turn to various communications sources to stay informed and obtain needed emergency evacuation information.

The Emergency Alert System (EAS) and the National Oceanic and Atmospheric Administration (NOAA) have established a communications network that continuously broadcasts weather, environmental, or technological danger by area. This network provides immediate broadcasting of warnings about impending earthquakes, tornadoes, floods, high winds, toxic chemical spills, or other public safety concerns.

The EAS system alerts are the warnings everyone receives on their TV sets. NOAA provides the weather information to the EAS automatically for communication over TV and radio. In those areas that do not receive EAS signals, NOAA will send alert information out on its own frequencies and also notify the appropriate TV and radio stations.

Weather and public alert information can also be received by a NOAA weather radio. These devices emit a loud audio warning signal, turn on a red warning indicator, display information on a small LCD screen, and provide an audio (radio) description of the dangerous condition. They are available both as small handheld radios (about $40) that run on C batteries and as small alarm clocks (about $30) that have both batteries and a 120-volt (AC) adapter. The weather radio is always on but stays dormant until activated by an alert. The advantage is that you do not have to tune to any specific station; a NOAA weather radio automatically monitors all pertinent EAS and NOAA frequencies.

We became believers in NOAA weather radios after an incident at the Yogi Bear's Jellystone Park Campground in Gardiner, New York. An EAS alert sounded on the weather radio in the campground store warning of the dangerously high winds and heavy rains that arrived within five minutes of the alert. We waited in the store until the rain stopped, and when we returned to our site we found that a large tree between our site and the neighboring site had split down the middle and dropped onto the site next to us. It completely covered the trailer, which was vacant at the time. In addition to that tree, six other large trees or limbs fell in the campground. Fortunately, the damage to our neighboring trailer was slight, and the other sites with fallen limbs and trees were vacant.

In addition to the NOAA weather radios, some portable radios and newer CBs have a "weather" channel or station that provides the weather information in the local area on a continuous basis. Weather channels don't provide the audio and visual warning signals in the event of dangerous weather or conditions given by the NOAA weather radios, but can be helpful to get local conditions.

Although these capabilities are important for all RVers, accurate understanding of potentially dangerous conditions is even more important for those who stay on the road for extended periods. We recommend all RVers take along a NOAA weather radio.

Dispatching the Laundry

Anyone gone from home more than two or three days will have to do laundry, or a lot of clothes shopping. The other, less desirable alternative is to just stay away from other people after a while. Most campgrounds have some restrictions on the types of laundry that can be hung outside the RV and the type of hanging device used. Check with the campground office about such issues, if you can't get an idea just by looking around at other sites. Our recommendation is to carry laundry supplies as follows:

— 1-quart bottles with tightly fitting caps can hold detergent, bleach, softener, and other liquid supplies.
— Plastic containers that can be opened or closed easily are a good way to transport powder products (detergent, baking soda, non-chlorine dry bleach, and other items).

All laundry items can be stowed in a small, plastic-covered bin big enough to hold all the supplies needed so that they can be retrieved quickly and transported to and from the laundry facility.

The use of containers and bins minimizes storage-space requirements, provides protection from spills, keeps the containers from bouncing around, and makes it easier to carry the supplies. Don't forget to bring a laundry basket or bag. We made a huge laundry bag that holds about six days' worth of laundry for two people. We leave it on the bathroom floor, because we are not fussy about such things. Others may want to stow dirty laundry somewhere else, such as in the compartment under the master-bedroom bed, which is probably the only inside area in most RVs that is big enough to hold a large bag of laundry.

We have the following suggestions regarding use of coin laundries:

- Buy a roll of quarters before you do your first load (the campground store always has lots of quarters, as the machines are emptied continuously throughout each day).
- Use the campground laundry if it's satisfactory (consider cleanliness, sufficient number of washers and dryers, water temperature and pressure, and price).
- Check out the laundry in the nearest community (you can do shopping, have lunch, or take a walk while the laundry is in the machines).
- Consider a laundry that will do the washing, drying, and folding for you. We have found during several trips in New York and New England that for 50–75 percent more, wash-dry-fold-hang laundries will do all the laundry tasks, including expert folding, the same day (and they use their own laundry detergent, bleach, and softener).
- If the campground laundry was unsatisfactory, tell the management when you leave (they may improve it for next year).

RVers with large rigs may want to consider installing a washer/dryer in the RV if space is available. The all-in-one units used in RVs cost approximately $1000 plus installation. They work very well, but the size of the wash load is smaller than that of a household washing machine, and many RVers find it necessary to use them on a daily basis. The combination washer/dryers come in two types: unvented and vented. Unvented machines use condensation for drying and moisture is pumped out through the drain hose. Vented machines dry clothes substantially faster because they exhaust the moisture through a vent to the outside. Some RVers use the washer/dryer while driving by running the generator.

For smaller rigs, the RVer may want to consider the small portable washing machine of the type used on boats. It is a small, sturdy plastic drum on a stand that holds up to 5 pounds of laundry and is turned with a small hand crank. It is available for approximately $35–$40 from RV, camping, and boating supply stores. You will have to wring out the clothes by hand, but the boat washers do a very good job of cleaning clothes.

You may also want to consider using a small folding clothes hanger or hook-on clothes pins (to hang over the bathtub or shower) for items washed by hand, for items washed in the portable machine described above, or just to dry out damp towels or clothing.

Computing on the Road

If you don't need one at home or the trip is short, you don't need one on the road. This section discusses the options you should consider if you decide to bring a computer. Chapter 1 (How to Find the Information You Need) describes internet sites to increase your RVing knowledge. The "RVs, Computers, and the Internet" section of Chapter 2 (Trip Planning That Works) provides more detailed information and resources to access the internet at home and on the road, and Chapter 10 (Keeping in Touch) covers your options for accessing the internet and sending and receiving e-mail.

If you enjoy using a computer at home, you may find it very helpful on extended trips. A personal computer (PC) can be used to pay bills, handle financial activities and transactions, plan trips, research possible routing and navigation, find information on the Web, and exchange e-mail on the internet.

Laptop or Desktop PC

You have your choice of a desktop machine or a laptop. We strongly recommend using a laptop PC because unless the campground or resort provides telephone lines at individual sites or you have a cellular phone link, you will have to carry your computer to the office, store, or clubhouse to connect to the internet. Laptop or notebook computers are smaller, lighter, and much more rugged than the desktop machines. Laptops can run on batteries, if you do not have an inverter or 120-volt (AC) power available, and are much better able to handle the vibration, bouncing, and jiggling of the RV.

When choosing a laptop or notebook computer, it is important to know the type of display used on any particular model. The active matrix or TFT type of display is more expensive but substantially brighter than the other displays. This is a critical factor if your copilot is using the laptop in the cab as you drive, while bright sunlight is streaming in. If you are purchasing a new laptop to be used in the RV, test the clarity, brightness, and visibility of the screen in the RV before completing the sale.

Power Considerations for Desktop PCs in RVs

If you want to bring a desktop PC, we recommend you review the use of an uninterruptible power supply (UPS) device or use an inverter with adequate power as described in the "RVs, Computers, and the Internet" section of Chapter 2 (Trip Planning That Works). These devices provide "clean" 120-volt (AC) power to prevent damage to your desktop PC from power failures and the power surges and low voltages common to many campgrounds and RV resorts. If you're using an inverter to power your desktop computer, make sure it has adequate power and outlets for any peripheral equipment (e.g., displays, printers, etc.) attached to your computer.

What Do You Need in Addition to the Computer?

We expect our machine to operate flawlessly on a trip. In the past three years, we had one problem, and it was a showstopper (we lost the entire contents of the hard drive). We recommend you bring the following:

— Operating system software on CD—you may need to load new drivers, update your software, or recover lost programs.

— Applications systems software on CD—you may need to load functions you don't use at home but need on the road.

— Several blank diskettes

- Portable Zip drive or CD-RW drive and appropriate blank diskettes and CDs for backups or storing digital pictures and other large files
- GPS tracking device for real-time navigation
- Computer user manual and copies of any information needed to get warranty service or repairs (when all else fails, the answer to the problem is frequently found in the manual)
- A small printer and paper—you may need paper copies of documents or lists. If you don't want to bring a printer, you can stop at any Kinko's and many print shops to print out computer files if necessary

With the exception of a printer and a CD-RW drive, all of the above should easily fit into a laptop computer bag along with the computer. As a reminder, Chapters 1, 2, and 10 provide additional information on the use of computers in your RV.

Taking Your Medicine

RVers will feel more confident if they have made plans in advance to ensure they have adequate medical, prescription, and dental services while traveling. Primary concerns may be availability of medical service providers, insurance coverage, and prescriptions.

RVers with serious or chronic illnesses should discuss their ability to travel and any appropriate limitations with their physician. They should discuss whether to bring a copy of all or part of their medical records and treatment plans on trips.

Availability of Medical Services

RVers should prepare a list of their current providers for medical, dental, and prescription services. They should then consider making a list of each travel destination and prepare a list of local providers they may need to contact for both continuing care and unanticipated emergencies. Both lists should be ready before leaving, and should be kept handy while traveling.

Health Insurance Coverage

RVers with insurance coverage through Health Medical Organizations (HMOs) or Preferred Provider Organizations (PPOs) should check to see what level of coverage is available outside of their home area.

HMOs and PPOs usually require you to contact them if you need coverage outside of your local area. It is important that you understand your insurer's coverage and the actions you must take to obtain covered treatment. Contact your HMO or PPO before your departure to inform them that you will be traveling and to confirm their procedures for out-of-area coverage.

Some plans (e.g., Aetna, Blue Cross/Blue Shield) extend coverage on a nationwide basis for travelers and will work with you to make arrangements for appropriate treatment. Others will only provide emergency treatment and then require you to return home for follow-up treatment.

Medical Evacuation and Assistance

RVers with serious or chronic health problems should consider the need for a medical evacuation and assistance policy that remains in effect while traveling. If your health plan or your personal needs require you to return home for unplanned medical treatment, investigate whether your plan has options to provide reimbursement for your transportation home, delivery of your RV to your home location, and temporary living and accommodations expenses. Coverage that pays for transportation needed to return home due to illness complications or incapacity is discussed further in Chapter 15 (Insurance, Road Service, Warranty Coverage, and Medical Evacuation).

Dental Insurance

RVers with insurance coverage through Dental Management Associations (DMAs) should check to see what level of coverage is available outside of their home area. Most DMAs (e.g., Delta, MetLife, and other providers) have nationwide coverage and have reimbursement policies for "in-plan" and "out-of-plan" dental services.

"In-plan" dentists and other dental providers can provide all services in their plan, generally at a slightly reduced fee. "Out-of-plan" dental practitioners may charge higher fees for dental procedures, and your out-of-pocket expenses may rise. If you need dental care on the road, the DMA will provide the telephone numbers and addresses of the nearest providers in their plan. They should advise you of "out-of-plan" provider reimbursement policies if they know no "in-plan" providers are available.

When seeking dental services on the road, it is important to contact the DMA before seeing a dentist and obtaining treatment. The reimbursement and coverage varies between the different dental plans for "in-plan" and "out-of-plan" providers. Some DMAs will not cover you for high-cost procedures if you use an "out-of-plan" provider when an "in-plan" provider was available.

Most DMAs request the dentist to submit a treatment plan for extensive or expensive dental services other than fillings and cleanings, such as crowns, bridges, or periodontal work. This allows them to preview needs before the procedures are performed. Unfortunately, most of them take at least two to four weeks to respond. If you need emergency treatment, such as getting a crown for a broken tooth, and can't wait for the DMA to respond, notify them that you are requesting an expedited review and that you are proceeding with the treatment.

Prescription Coverage

RVers on extended trips should bring their prescription medications with them, but most of the major drug stores (e.g., Walgreens, Eckerd, CVS, etc.) will allow you to obtain refills at any of their stores in the country.

We always obtain refill prescriptions from our doctor before leaving on an extended trip. Some national chains allow you to fill the prescriptions in locations throughout the United States. You can leave them with your home pharmacy if it is a national chain with stores in your destination areas. Otherwise, bring prescriptions with you, especially if you anticipate using local pharmacies or there are no major chain pharmacies at your destinations.

It is important that you bring an adequate supply of your prescription medications with you if you are traveling in Mexico or Canada. You will need a local doctor's prescription in those countries to obtain medications. The national chains cannot issue medications in Canada or Mexico from a prescription written by a U.S. physician.

Cool- and Cold-Weather RVing

Many RVers take to the road in the early spring to enjoy the early blooming or to kick off the fishing season, in the fall to enjoy the changing foliage or the hunting season, and in the winter to enjoy skiing, snowmobiling, ice skating, or ice fishing. Of course, visiting friends and relatives is part of these activities, especially over holiday periods. RVing in cool and cold weather requires you to do some extra planning to protect the RV against the cold and to help find economical ways to heat the interior.

Protecting the RV

It is extremely important that you have the proper amount of antifreeze in the engine cooling system and that you are following the manufacturer recommendations for cold-weather operation of diesel-powered engines and generators. Diesel engines require modified fuels and preheating for winter use. If you will be driving a diesel-powered RV from a warm climate to a cold climate, make sure you have the correct diesel fuels for the areas you are driving through.

In addition to antifreeze and fuel, it's important for the engine and coach batteries to be in good condition for cold-weather camping. Ensure that all battery terminals are clean, all cables are tight, the cells are filled to the correct level, and the electrolyte is at the correct pH level. While in campgrounds, you may want to start the engine up in the late afternoon for a short period of time to ensure everything is working and to create some residual heat under the coach.

It is also necessary to keep the RV interior, storage and equipment bays, fresh water tank, holding tanks, and hot water heater from freezing. You can install thermostatically controlled tank heaters on your holding tanks. They are rated to protect tanks of up to 40 gallons from freezing and are available from Camping World and other RV suppliers in either 12-volt (DC) or 110-volt (AC)/ 12-volt (DC) power-source models. We recommend the AC/DC power-source model to allow you to use your coach batteries on the road and the 110-volt (AC) power when you're in a campground.

If you are in the process of buying a new RV and plan on cold-weather use, you may want to consider the following features:

- Increased RV wall thickness and insulation rating
- A hot water heater that runs on either 110 volts (AC), propane, or both (running on electricity alone is less efficient but saves on propane)
- Dual or thermopane windows to improve the efficiency of the RV heating system by reducing heat loss
- Heated and insulated storage bays
- Heated and insulated holding tanks, fresh water tank, and associated plumbing lines
- Rear bedroom heat exchanger and fan to heat the RV bedroom while driving
- Hot water–tank heat exchanger to preheat the RV hot water while driving

These features are very important in the winter when the temperature difference between inside and outside may be 60 degrees.

Bring the appropriate cold-weather coats, sweaters, hats, and gloves, as well as extra blankets, comforters, and flannel sheets.

Pick a site with as much protection from the wind as possible. High winds create a low windchill factor, which requires additional energy to heat the RV.

The windshield is a major loss of heat. We recommend that you use your windshield sunshade and close all your drapes and shades in the RV to help retain heat and reduce drafts.

A second loss of heat in the RV is the exhaust fans in the bath and kitchen areas. There are a number of inexpensive vent shields available from RV supply stores to reduce heat loss through the fan assemblies. Make sure that no fans get turned on while the opening is covered. If you get a moisture buildup from the bath area or kitchen area, you may have to periodically remove a cover vent for a brief time.

Another option for those in cool or cold climates is to replace or cover the screen in the screen door with clear vinyl, creating a "storm door" to help keep in heat.

To reduce the incidence of freezing pipes, plan on wrapping insulation around your fresh water hose, fixture, and everything above ground level when you are connecting to city water if there is any possibility the temperature may go below freezing.

If your black and gray water holding tanks are not in a protected, insulated, and heated area and you don't have holding tank heaters, you should be prepared to do the following if you anticipate the temperature going below freezing:

— Add RV antifreeze to both holding tanks.

— Connect 3-inch sewer hose to drain tanks.

— Rinse, remove, and store sewer hose in insulated storage bay after draining tanks.

If your RV's fresh water holding tank is in a protected, insulated, and heated area, our recommendation in cold weather is to fill the fresh water tank, disconnect and drain your water supply hose, and store it in a heated and insulated bay when it is not in use. Check the area of the tank to make sure the temperature remains above freezing. You should have a spare hose in the event your primary hose becomes damaged or blocked from icing up.

A Lidstone Law of RVing: Never use your stove or oven or any heater that requires oxygen from inside the RV for heating. This is an extremely dangerous and possibly deadly practice. Such appliances can deplete the oxygen in the RV, resulting in serious injury or death to the occupants.

If you leave your water hose connected, you should turn off the outside water supply and drain your water supply hose to the RV whenever you leave the RV.

Heating the RV Interior

The first line of defense is the propane-powered gas furnace. These furnaces can normally generate anywhere from 25,000 to 40,000 BTUs of heat and up. The heated air is normally distributed using the floor and wall vents. You know it's working because of the loud sucking noise, which is your propane fuel being burned. Keep in mind that the efficiency of the propane furnace drops as the outside temperature drops. Be sure to make the necessary preparations to obtain additional propane while you are away from home.

To help save propane, you can consider using other additional RV heating options such as the Duo-Therm heat pump manufactured by Dometic instead of the standard roof air-conditioning system unit. The heat pump enables you to obtain approximately 12,000 BTUs of heat from each roof unit. The heated air is distributed through the air-conditioning ducting and vents. The heat pumps cost approximately $200 more than standard air-conditioning units, but you will save money on propane if you do cold-weather camping.

If you have standard roof air-conditioning units (Coleman or Duo-Therm), you may be able to install a 5,600 BTU heat strip in each unit. These are basically toaster elements. As with heat pumps, the heated air is distributed through the air-conditioning ducting and vents.

Propane-powered catalytic heaters with 5,000–6,000 BTUs of heating capacity are available for use in vented areas. *Do not use a catalytic heater in any unvented area because the catalytic heater consumes oxygen.*

Another option is a small, portable electric heater, which generates approximately 1,500 watts of heat. These are basically fan-powered toasters and cost $20–$50. Technology varies between models, and they are very effective in taking the chill out of the air on cool mornings.

Electric blankets will allow you to remain warm while sleeping if the heating systems are having difficulty keeping the RV warm enough or you would like to turn the thermostat to a lower setting at night. You can also buy polar fleece in 60-inch widths and cut the fleece into suitable lengths for use as blankets. It won't ravel and it's warm! You can also trim up the fleece lengths to make them more fancy if you are handy with a needle and sewing machine or glue gun.

Going Home

Check the actual and forecasted outside air temperatures both in the area you're visiting and in the locations along your route home. Driving an RV at 50–60 miles per hour creates a very low windchill factor, which can freeze exposed tanks or plumbing very quickly if the outside temperature is below freezing.

If your fresh water tank and internal plumbing lines are not adequately protected, insulated, or heated to prevent damage from freezing, and the outside temperatures are below freezing, be prepared to do the following before leaving for home:

- Drain the fresh water system and related appliances or add RV anti-freeze.
- Drain the black and gray water holding tanks and add odor-control chemicals, water, and RV antifreeze.

If you will be driving a diesel-powered RV from a cold climate to a warmer climate, make sure that you have the correct diesel fuels for the areas you are driving through.

- - - - - -

CHAPTER 4

VISITING NATIONAL, STATE, AND COUNTY PARKS

We have found national, state, and county parks to be wonderful places for RVers to experience the beauty of nature's magnificent vistas. The combination of scenic vistas, nature and ecology, historical sites, and sports and recreational opportunities put these facilities high up on your RVing list of places to go or visit—you are already helping pay for them, so you might as well use them!

National Parks

The national parks represent an incredible recreational opportunity for RVers, whether north or south of the Mason–Dixon line, or east or west of the Mississippi River. The national parks vary in size from an acre or two to hundreds of thousands of acres in urban, suburban, rural, undeveloped, and wilderness areas. All are a pleasure to visit and renew our pride as stewards of the land.

National parks are a great place to RV and are a super bargain because everyone can obtain a reasonable rate. For instance, senior citizens qualify for the Golden Age Passport and younger visitors can purchase the Golden Eagle Passport.

An excellent book on national parks is *National Geographic's Guide to the National Parks of the United States*, which covers fifty-four parks and includes extensive maps, photographs, and related information.

Although many of the national parks are in the West, there is one in the Virgin Islands and a series of them from Florida to Maine.

National Parks and Federal Lands Websites and Telephone Numbers

The following is a partial list of the websites that feature information related to national parks and federal lands:

Agency	Website
USDA Forest Service	www.fs.fed.us
National Park Service	www.nps.gov
National Recreation Reservation Service—reservation service for 1,700 locations managed by the USDA Forest Service and the U.S. Army Corps of Engineers	www.reserveusa.com
Commercial website—extensive information on outdoor recreation and national parks	www.gorp.com

Discounted Entrance Fees for National Parks

Those living near or traveling to areas with a national park can take advantage of various programs that provide reduced fees for entrance to national parks and other federal sites. Examples are:

- Golden Eagle Passport—This is a yearly pass that costs $50 and provides admittance to all occupants of a vehicle.
- Golden Age Passport—Persons who are sixty-two or older can obtain this pass at a cost of $10. It is valid for a lifetime and provides admittance to all occupants of a vehicle.
- Golden Access Passport—Disabled persons can obtain the Golden Access Passport free of charge. This is a lifetime pass that provides admittance to all occupants of a vehicle.

The passports can normally be obtained at any national park that charges fees and off the National Park Service website. An additional benefit is that selected states and other federal facilities may honor the passes and provide discounts for camping and entering facilities.

State Parks

Every state in the Union provides and maintains state parks that furnish extensive facilities and services to hikers, campers, and RVers. Each state provides extensive information about the state park systems, maps, and area attractions and services. Sources of information include internet sites, toll-free telephone numbers, and brochures and materials provided at the Interstate Highway System welcome stations and visitor centers. Many RVers visit the beautiful state parks even when staying at private or municipal campgrounds and RV resorts.

The rates for camping at state parks are very reasonable (some parks offer reduced campground fees to senior citizens), but campsite services and RV site sizes often have limitations. Even so, the state parks provide many varied and excellent recreational facilities. RVers can go fishing in the spring, go swimming in oceans and lakes, and go boating in the summer. Additionally, one can go hunting in the fall and go skiing in the winter, and go hiking year-round.

Although state park campsites frequently are only 35–40 feet in length, the campgrounds are generally more heavily treed and spread out, providing more privacy. One of the most beautiful campsites we have had yet was a tent site in Big Basin Redwoods State Park west of Saratoga, California. The site was about 80 feet by 100 feet under towering redwoods. It was more like a cathedral than a campsite. RVers should find out what hookups are available, because water and electricity are generally available in many state parks, but sewer hookups tend to be very limited.

The state parks are included in all the major campground directories by geographic location. We recommend that you use your campground directories to determine the specific hookup services (electricity, water, and sewer) available at each state park you are interested in visiting. In addition, check the beginning of each state listing in your Woodall's campground directory because some of the states have provided a short descriptive listing of state parks and campgrounds. The Trailer Life campground directory has a listing of all the state tourist bureaus with phone numbers and websites.

State Park Websites and Telephone Numbers

Each of the states has a website that provides information about its state parks, forests, and preserves. The individual state websites provide substantial information, but presentation and links to other sites differ from state to state. Most state websites only provide links to other locations on their own sites, but a few provide links to national parks, federal lands, or private campgrounds. These sites also tend to be very sketchy regarding specific campground information and services other than fees and reservation contacts. Therefore, you will still need to consult a campground directory that provides more detail about the specific state campground of interest.

Some states have toll-free numbers for making reservations at all state parks within the entire state, but many states will advise you to contact the individual state park. Keep in mind that many state parks charge a nonrefundable fee for reservations.

State park websites and related information are listed by state in Appendix A.

County Parks

County parks are the "sleepers" of the campgrounds and resorts. They tend to be very casual and relaxing places to stay, with excellent recreational facilities and the advantage of very reasonable fees. The county and municipal campgrounds tend to close down their offices earlier than privately run campgrounds. Also, because most county campgrounds are located in parks and nature preserves, they may lock the entrances at closing time. We suggest you ask what time the campground store/office closes when you make your reservations. It's also a good idea to ask about the campground's procedure for late arrivals, particularly if there is a gate that gets locked at night. We have always been able to easily obtain the information or assistance necessary to gain entrance after closing hours.

We've enjoyed visiting the Campground at James Island, South Carolina, several times. This county park contains a 640-acre water and nature preserve, as well as a campground with approximately 200 large, scenic, and well-maintained sites. James Island has a friendly staff and runs shuttles to Folly Beach, a popular local ocean beach on the Atlantic. Attractions abound nearby; the campground is about five minutes from golf and shopping, and visitors can drive to downtown Charleston in about ten minutes to enjoy its many restaurants, shops, and historic sites and homes.

CHAPTER 5

ENTERING CANADA AND MEXICO

Crossing the border to go outside the United States in your RV is not identical to crossing a state line. In this chapter you will learn how to make your stay more pleasant (and legal) when visiting our neighbors to the north and south.

RVers must ensure that they have the appropriate documents to enter Canada and Mexico and return to the United States. Border-crossing RVers should also have a full understanding of the unique requirements our neighbors expect of visitors.

Campgrounds in Canada are very similar to those in the United States because most campgrounds have all the required hookups. Campgrounds in Mexico are more rugged and may not have compatible or even adequate services and resources. For instance, many campgrounds in Mexico have only 15 amp or 10 amp electrical service and limited sewer service. RVers must be prepared to use their generator sets on a regular basis in Mexico. Also, we suggest that you keep all outside storage compartments and engine access locked at all times. Unlock them only to remove or store items or to service the RV.

Canada

Visitors to Canada should carry copies of their vehicle registration, proof of insurance, and proof of citizenship (birth certificate, passport, draft card, military ID card, or voter registration card). If you are a temporary resident of the United States or a visitor from any other country, you will require a passport to enter Canada. Permanent U.S. residents who have legal resident alien status should bring their alien registration receipt card when entering Canada. Although you may not be requested to show the ID documents when entering Canada, they may be required if you need medical care or become involved in an accident while in Canada, or when you return to the United States.

Pets

U.S. citizens and residents can bring dogs and cats into Canada without quarantine restrictions. Dogs more than eight months of age require a valid rabies certificate issued by a licensed veterinarian from the country of origin that clearly identifies the dogs and shows that they were vaccinated against rabies at least once within the preceding three-year period.

Cats more than three months of age have the same certification requirements as dogs. Vaccination is not required if the dog or cat is less than three months of age. For other pets, including birds, turtles and tortoises, and so forth, contact the Canadian Food Inspection Agency for further details and requirements.

Insurance

Canada requires all motor vehicles, including RVs, to carry liability insurance. Canada accepts the coverage of any vehicle registered and insured in the United States. You can also obtain a Canadian Nonresident Interprovincial Motor Vehicle Liability Insurance Card from your U.S. insurer as additional proof of insurance.

Guns

Canada is very strict about guns (as well as illicit drugs). Bringing handguns or automatic firearms into Canada is illegal, and the penalties are rigorous. Rifles and shotguns with barrels longer than 18.5 inches are permissible, but they must be declared and stored in the proper manner.

Gas and Diesel Fuel

Gas and diesel fuel are readily available but substantially more expensive in Canada than in the United States. We suggest you top off your RV and toad fuel tanks before entering Canada.

Banking and Money Exchange

You can exchange U.S. dollars for Canadian dollars at any bank and most businesses, or obtain Canadian currency at any ATM machine in Canada.

To avoid coming back to the United States with a lot of leftover Canadian bills and coins, we recommend the use of your ATM or debit card at ATM machines for "walking-around money" as you need it. When using the ATM machine, check that any fees for use of the machine are reasonable.

Debit and credit cards are advised for all other expenses (restaurants, campgrounds, service stations, etc.); they are convenient and may also get you a better exchange rate.

Groceries

Canada has few restrictions on the importation of most prepackaged meat and dairy products, preprocessed food products, and condiments carried for personal consumption. In addition, most common produce products may be brought across the border from the United States. It is important to advise the customs personnel of the types of food and alcohol products you are bringing across the border. They will advise you of any problem foods. You can bring in up to 40 ounces of liquor per person, 1.5 liters of wine per person, and twenty-four 12-ounce cans of beer per person.

Although Canada is very similar to the United States, we found food shopping to be a little different, depending on where you go. You may encounter new brand names, different names for cuts of meat, and a slightly different variety of food products. If you're not familiar with the area you plan to visit, make sure you have adequate stocks of food and beverages before you arrive. While visiting the Headquarters Campground in Fundy National Park in Alma, New Brunswick, the nearest supermarkets we could find were more than an hour away (38 miles south to Sussex, or 49 miles north to Moncton).

TV

Cable access is very limited in many areas of Canada. In Fundy National Park we could only receive two channels using the antenna. The only guarantee of TV programming is a satellite dish antenna and an RV site with no trees blocking the line of sight for the antenna.

Mexico

Visitors to Mexico should carry original copies of their proof of citizenship (birth certificate, passport, or voter registration card), driver license, copies of vehicle insurance policies, and original vehicle titles in the name of the person driving the vehicle. If there is a lienholder on a vehicle, an original notarized letter of permission to take the vehicle into Mexico is required. If you are a legal alien in the United States and wish to enter Mexico and return to the United States, you may need to verify your ability to return with the Immigration and Naturalization Service (INS).

Touring Mexico

The recommended way to tour Mexico is with an RV group and caravan. Traveling in bunches provides more security, and the tour guides are familiar enough with the campgrounds, locales, and language to ensure that the trip will be enjoyable and without any unpleasant surprises.

There is a possibility that you could pass through military or police checkpoints as you travel through Mexico. Police personnel may check both the RV interior and outside storage bays, while checking for the proper insurance, documents, and contraband. Be respectful and courteous at these checkpoints. Have your ID documents and vehicle registration, title, Mexican tourist permits, and insurance papers ready and answer all questions in a direct and straightforward manner. In addition, you may also pass through agricultural checkpoints where inspectors check for food and plants; the inspectors may spray the undercarriage of the RV, and they may charge a small fee if they spray insecticide or disinfectant.

In Mexico, RV service, including coach systems, power plant, and chassis, as well as parts availability, may be substantially limited compared to the United States and Canada. In addition, RVers may experience somewhat lengthy delays to obtain spare parts. Conceivably, these delays could become part of your vacation, but the likelihood of this happening is minimal.

Before entering Mexico, we recommend that some specific RV service and maintenance tasks be completed. For instance, the RV and generator service should be up-to-date. You should also make sure that RV operation, use, and maintenance documents are available and current. The tool set, hydraulic jack, and air compressor should be in good working order and readily available, and a sufficient, extra quantity of engine oil and hydraulic fluid should be stowed in one of the RV's bays. Spare air filters and oil for the generator should also be on board when entering Mexico.

Required Additional Liability Insurance

Mexico requires vehicles from the United States to carry liability insurance coverage from a Mexican insurance company. Your U.S. insurance is not sufficient for driving in Mexico, and failure to carry the required liability insurance coverage issued by a valid Mexican insurance carrier is a felony in Mexico. In addition, you may also have to purchase property damage, medical payments, legal aid, collision, and comprehensive coverage from a Mexican insurance carrier. RVers should also understand that Mexican police are empowered to impound any vehicle involved in an accident.

A Lidstone Law of RVing: Check your insurance coverage requirements and status with both your U.S. vehicle insurer and the agency issuing the Mexican vehicle insurance coverage before driving into Mexico to make sure you have the necessary bodily injury liability, property damage, medical payments, legal aid, collision, and comprehensive coverage for the areas you plan to visit.

The cost of thirty days' coverage in Mexico can get expensive; at least $200 for a late-model auto and $800 for an RV. The cost is dependent on the number of days you will be in Mexico and the value of your vehicles. We recommend you contact your U.S. insurer to obtain names of carriers or insurance agencies that can provide the necessary Mexican vehicle coverage for both your RV and your toad.

Guns

Bringing guns into Mexico is illegal and the offense is almost always prosecuted. You will go to jail and incur very expensive legal costs if you are arrested for bringing guns into Mexico for any reason. You will stay in jail for a minimum of several months while the charges are being resolved, and the

U.S. government will not help you (other than to verify your U.S. citizenship or legal resident alien status).

Banking and Money Exchange

You can exchange U.S. currency for Mexican pesos at any bank. However, bank hours vary, and you may encounter long lines. The easiest way to obtain Mexican pesos is to use your ATM or debit card at ATM machines. Contact your card issuers before leaving for Mexico to verify their coverage in Mexico. Visa and MasterCard are generally available worldwide. When using an ATM machine, check that any fees for use of the machine are reasonable.

As in Canada, we recommend using debit or credit cards for your primary expenses (restaurants, campgrounds, service stations, etc.), for convenience and the ability to get a better exchange rate.

Groceries and Water

Food shopping is significantly different in Mexico, but the food is one reason that RVers enjoy touring there. Use caution and common sense when buying food, and be sure to clean it very well and cook it properly.

We recommend that you fill your fresh water tank before entering Mexico and bring plenty of bottled water. Make sure any local water going into your fresh water holding tank is not contaminated or untreated. Also, be aware that the natural bacteria strains found in all water may be different in Mexico and may upset your stomach.

We suggest you use a high-quality water filter/purification system that will remove chlorine and as many chemicals, microbes, bacteria, and other contaminants as possible from all drinking and cooking water. A variety of effective water filtration systems that install under the sink or at the fresh water hookup are available from RV equipment suppliers and Camping World.

We strongly recommend that RVers "superchlorinate" or purify all Mexican water added to the fresh water holding tank. You can chlorinate your water by adding 1 teaspoon ($\frac{1}{6}$ of an ounce) of ordinary household liquid chlorine bleach, such as Clorox, for each 10 gallons of water in the holding tank.

One convenient way to do this is to attach the fresh water hose to the RV fitting, add the chlorine at the faucet end of the hose, attach the hose to the water faucet, and fill the tank. This will disinfect the supply hose as well as add the proper amount of chlorine to the tank. Your water filter/purification system will remove all or most of the chlorine as you use the water, so that the taste is not affected.

CHAPTER 6

MAKING SURE THE RV IS READY TO ROLL

Even though the word "maintenance" conjures up the specter of work, this chapter can streamline and speed up maintenance chores. A quick overview of the importance of RV maintenance, who does it, and key checkpoints to review before hitting the road will help any RVer understand the reason for maintenance.

For instance, taking off in an RV that is in poor condition may result in unplanned breakdowns and expenses and a spoiled RV trip. Our RVs represent a major investment of dollars, time, and effort to us. Keeping your RV properly maintained helps protect your investment, helps you sleep well at night, prevents breakdowns that cause trip delays and repair costs, and lengthens the maximum service life of your RV.

Warranty conditions are another very good and very important reason to maintain your RV. Warranty coverage may require proof of satisfactory completion of stipulated maintenance when warranty-covered claims are filed. Service and restitution may be denied in the event of an equipment failure if required maintenance cannot be proven or demonstrated for a covered item or system.

RV Service Providers

RV maintenance and service can be performed by one or more of the following service providers:

— The owner
— RV dealerships
— RV service shops and facilities
— Factory-authorized repair and service facilities
— Chassis and power train manufacturer service shops

Choice of service providers depends on the complexity of the task, the skill of the person or facility performing the maintenance, whether the work requires warranty coverage, and when the shop can complete the necessary work.

The RV service model that most of us are familiar with is to have coach maintenance and warranty service provided by factory-authorized RV dealers. The chassis and power train maintenance, service, and warranty service available is provided by the chassis and power train—manufacturer service facilities.

Recently, some of the chassis and power train manufacturers such as GM (workhorse chassis), Spartan, and Freightliner have been authorizing RV dealers with the proper service facilities to provide all necessary maintenance and warranty services for the chassis and power train. This is a major improvement because it provides a true one-stop shopping opportunity for your RV service and warranty needs. This new service arrangement should soothe your RVer concerns that you could get whipsawed by an RV dealer saying it was a chassis problem and the chassis manufacturer service shop saying it was an RV/coach problem.

We Lidstones, who are mere RV owners, have found that we can perform many preventive maintenance tasks ourselves, which saves a lot of money. For warranty work and most work that could affect the warranty, we make appointments with RV World, the dealer that sold us our RV. Dealers have excellent working relationships with manufacturers, (extended) warranty providers, and parts providers. We also use the nearby Ford heavy-truck dealer because Ford is the chassis provider.

Keep in mind that RV dealers continuously stay very busy preparing new, recently sold RVs for pickup by their new owners. Therefore, you could have to factor in short or long delays when scheduling service appointments for routine service or repairs. Fortunately, we also have an excellent local RV service shop that provides both extensive services (including engine rebuild) and generally quick turnaround, and also works with the extended warranty companies. All RV owners should have contingency plans and access to alternate service providers for preventive and scheduled RV maintenance services.

Many RV service shops and organizations are subject to seasonal workloads. Don't wait until the last minute to try to schedule service. We advise contacting your service provider well ahead of your trips to inquire about the shop's scheduling needs and the availability of any necessary factory parts and supplies. This allows the shop to complete the work in a timely way, thus allowing you to avoid situations where trip schedules and reservations have to be changed, or your loading time is shortened.

Types of RV Service

RV service activities fall into three broad categories:

- Preventive maintenance
- Coach scheduled service (everything installed on the chassis by the RV manufacturer)
- Chassis and power train scheduled service for motorhomes (chassis, engine, transmission, steering, suspension and braking systems, etc.)

Always perform the preventive maintenance tasks covered in Chapter 17 (Preventive Maintenance) to eliminate or reduce the number of situations or breakdowns that result in unscheduled repairs or road service. We do most of our own preventive maintenance because it doesn't require special tools, extensive time, or training. Some maintenance tasks are very simple but very important. For instance, the various coach systems must be started up or run about once a month. These include the air-conditioning system, furnace system, generator, water pump and heater, leveling system, and slideouts. Operating these devices and systems ensures that they are operating properly. The same applies to the motorhome engine, transmission, air-conditioning, and heater.

Be sure to take the time to carefully read your coach and chassis manuals, as well as the booklets and information provided by the various makers of the RV systems installed in your RV. The instructions and diagrams are excellent and cover important information regarding maintenance, troubleshooting, and service activities for just about everything installed in your coach and chassis. In addition, Bob Livingston's *RV Repair and Maintenance Manual,* published by Trailer Life, is an excellent source of information for new and experienced RVers and is readily available from bookstores, Camping World stores, and RV supply stores. It is a comprehensive guide to preventive and scheduled RV maintenance needs, troubleshooting and repair instructions, and toad towing considerations and requirements.

One of the objectives of our book is to inform fellow RVers that they can safely and easily complete many preventive maintenance tasks themselves. Proactive maintenance by the owner/RVer can be done if the owner keeps in mind that maintenance must be done in accordance with procedures recommended and required under the conditions of the warranty. Do-it-yourselfers can reduce RV expenses, identify problems before they result in expensive repairs or breakdowns, get a better understanding of how everything works, and keep the RV looking good and running smoothly. However, if you are unable or reluctant to perform a specific task, then refer the job to a professional.

We believe that preventive maintenance is cheaper than repair and can prevent breakdowns on the road. We know that some percentage of repairs and breakdowns on the road are the result of neglected preventive maintenance and scheduled service activity.

Before You Hit the Road

Before leaving for an RV trip, irrespective of the duration or distance of the trip, the following procedures should be completed by the owner or qualified service provider:

— Check the tires (including the spare) for age, wear, and correct tire pressure. All RV industry groups agree that tires should be replaced when showing wear or sun or age defects. The maximum life of tires, regardless of wear or other damage, is five to seven years. There is no such thing as a "safe" blowout of a tire. If a front tire goes, the driver will have major steering and control problems affecting their ability to safely stop the RV and get it off the road. When a rear tire blows, it is invariably an inside tire that will require even more time and work for you or your road service.

— Complete any outstanding preventive maintenance checks, as discussed in detail in Chapter 17. These tasks do not take long to complete, can normally be done by the RVer, and require minimum tools and supplies.

— Complete any scheduled service actions coming due—such as lube and oil change, tire rotation, brake service, or transmission service—or make arrangements to have them done on the road as required. The scheduled RV service activities are discussed in the "Scheduled and Major Mainte-nance Needs" section in Chapter 17. Don't forget to complete any necessary service for your toad, tow-bar system, car dolly, or boat or auto trailer before you hit the road.

— Check the tow bar, mounting brackets, trailer hitch, pins, safety chains, and connections carefully for cracks, frayed wiring, loose connections, rust, or any other damage that affects safety.

Don't Forget the RV Documents

We always carry the RV operation, use, and maintenance documents in the RV whenever we're on the road. These documents should be the first line of defense if operational or mechanical problems arise with the RV or its systems.

These documents became very important on one of our trips when the slideout would not retract fully. We were saved by the manufacturer's trou-bleshooting instructions, which enabled us to retract a jammed slideout sufficiently to travel until we could get our RV into a repair facility.

You should also carry a copy of your warranties and extended warranty contracts in the RV whenever it's on the road.

CHAPTER 7

WHAT GOES IN THE RV?

The most tedious part of RVing can be loading and unloading the rig, so we provide some suggestions on how to make it easier. Because we require space to store equipment and personal effects, and fuel to carry them, we recommend that you carefully consider the weight, how compactly items can be stored, and the total volume required when selecting items to take on your trips.

The adage "a place for everything, and everything in its place" is especially telling for RVers who want to enjoy extended trips. Our recommendations on what, where, and when to stow everything you need can help you spend more time enjoying yourself and less time tracking down necessities and other supplies.

Where Do You Put Everything?

The type and length of the RV determines the amount of storage capacity in the coach and outside compartments. Motorhomes generally have more storage than recreational trailers and fifth-wheels. Class A motorhomes, which usually have basement compartment storage, have the most storage overall because their length can be up to 45 feet.

The inside storage of the RV holds the same types of personal, clothing, bath, and kitchen items stored inside your permanent home. Combinations of drawers, cabinets, and closets are provided for your living needs.

Outside storage is used for RV support and recreational needs, including tools, safety equipment, utility hookups, and comfort items. Usage is based on total capacity and how you use your RV. The length of time away from home and distances traveled may affect what you carry.

And when you get done considering how to use the space in the RV, there may also be space available in the toad. It's ideal for large bulky items like golf clubs or picnic coolers that you want ready access to, but seem awkward to put in bays. Any items that will be transported in the car at the destination can also travel in the car while it is being towed.

For the bathroom items (or other items to be stored in small or shallow spaces), we've had great success using 1-inch-thick foam padding to cover all items in the medicine chest to keep them from rattling, rolling around, or breaking. The foam padding is readily available in most craft stores. We cut it to a size slightly larger than the opening so it doesn't fall out when the door is opened and stow it under the sink when we reach our destination. You can also buy nonslip rubber liners (available in rolls and precut sizes) from RV supply stores such as Camping World. Placing the liner material on the bottom of all cabinets and drawers helps to keep the contents from sliding around (as well as reducing scratching and wear).

Consider using large, lightweight plastic bins to hold items being put into the storage bays. Rigid, solid-sided bins and plastic milk crates (which can be found in office supply superstores) will help keep the bays neat. Items stored in bins and crates also do not slide around the carpeted storage areas. Put similar items together and stow containers that are opened frequently near the point where they are used. For instance, it's a good idea to store the water hose, sewer hoses and fittings, and power cords near their connections.

We recommend putting the sewer hoses and fittings in large plastic garbage bags within the appropriate storage box or bins to reduce any odors. Replace the bags when they rip or start to retain odors.

Loading Up

We recommend loading the RV on the day prior to your departure, especially if you plan to drive more than three or four hours the first day. For extended trips, with lots of stuff, you may want to spread it over two or three days. The experience of most RVers is that it becomes easier with each trip (same amount of time, but less worrying about forgetting things). Most forgotten items are easily restocked from shopping centers, supermarkets, and campgrounds during the trip.

In addition to food, clothing, and personal items, RVers also need to have support items on board. These include tools, safety and breakdown equipment, hookup items, and entertainment and housekeeping items. Most of these can be left in the RV because they're needed on most trips.

When items used only for the RV are stored permanently in the RV's bays, the time and effort required to load your RV for a trip is shortened. You will only have to haul food, clothing, personal items, and other support items out to the RV.

To help make sure we don't miss anything, we always consult and use our checklist. The checklist is simply a PC word-processor–created document consisting of one huge table. The table has columns that list every possible item we might need on RV trips (short, medium, and long) with a space alongside each item for a check mark. The items on the checklist are organized into columns depending upon where the various items are located in our home (e.g., kitchen, bathroom, bedroom). A sample checklist is contained in Appendix D.

We use the checklist in a two-step mode. The first step is to help decide what to bring on the trip and cross out the items we don't need. The second is to review the list again as we load the RV. For shorter trips, we still go through the entire checklist. Using a checklist is recommended because checking off necessities will ensure that specific items needed on a trip are not forgotten. For instance, we can easily check off "shorts" and "swimsuits" in the summer, and cross out "sweaters" and "warm jackets" until we plan to take off on a cooler-weather trip.

There are three rules to remember about everything loaded into your RV:
- Every item adds weight, which requires you to burn fuel to carry it.
- Many of the items loaded into the RV at the start of the trip have to be unloaded at the end of the trip.
- If you don't plan to use an item, don't bring it (e.g., if you aren't carrying bicycles, leave the bike rack in the garage).

The time required to load up your RV is affected by the length of time you will be traveling. Longer trips may require more types of clothing, more recreational items, and more food and kitchen items. Don't forget to turn on the RV refrigerator twelve to twenty-four hours before loading food into it.

What Else Goes in Besides Food and Clothing?

Traveling on the road requires a variety of support items to make the trip more enjoyable and to attend to any necessary maintenance or minor repairs. As we mentioned above, a lot of these items can be left in the RV on a permanent basis because you will need them on every trip.

The support items are broken down into the following categories:

— Tools
— Safety and breakdown equipment
— Hookup items
— Recreation and leisure items
— Housekeeping and miscellaneous items

We suggest you review the following lists of these support items to determine which seem most applicable to your RV trip. The specific items to be carried may vary depending on the amount of interior and exterior storage space, distance to be traveled, location, and time away from home.

Tools

Having the proper tools and safety equipment on board will help you perform preventive maintenance and selected scheduled maintenance tasks in a professional and safe manner. Because most tools are inexpensive, we recommend that you leave a set in the RV. Stow the tools permanently in an external compartment close to the RV's entrance door. We purchased most of ours in discount and home repair stores such as Kmart, Wal-Mart, Big Lots, and Home Depot.

Suggested items to be considered for your RV toolbox include:

— Flashlights (see note below)
— Hammer
— Rubber mallet
— Slotted screwdriver
— Phillips screwdriver
— Hex wrench set

- $^3/_8$-inch and $^1/_4$-inch socket set, including a $^3/_8$- to-$^1/_2$-inch adapter
- Adjustable wrench
- Pliers
- Electric drill and drill set
- Air compressor with cord capable of reaching all wheels, including those on the towed vehicle
- Work gloves
- Safety glasses
- Spare lightbulbs for coach and vehicle
- Silicone spray
- Silicone adhesive
- WD-40
- Kwik-Lube
- Spare wrench or appropriate socket to tighten or release the car dolly straps (if you use a car dolly)

Safety/Breakdown Equipment to Store Inside the RV

We suggest you store these items in storage compartments close to both the driver and the passenger:

- Air pressure gauge (see note below)
- Spare fuses (automotive and coach)
- Cellular phone, 12-volt (DC) charger, and 120-volt (AC) charger
- Maps
- Flashlights and batteries
- Fire extinguishers
- Weather-alert radio
- CB radio
- Two large fold-up ponchos for bad weather (in addition to the usual inclement-weather gear and umbrellas)

A Lidstone Law of RVing:
Always bring at least one "snake" flashlight.
A "snake light" is a must-have for RVers because its flexibility leaves both of your hands free to perform tasks in tight spaces.
The snake light can be draped around your neck when lying on your back, or you can set it on the ground or wrap it around another object when attaching hookups or checking out problems. Snake lights are available in hardware stores, home improvement stores, and superstores.

- Spare batteries for smoke and carbon monoxide detectors
- Phone numbers for emergency contacts, doctors, pharmacies, medical service providers, and road service
- RV registration and proof of insurance
- RV warranty and extended warranty coverage
- RV manuals and documents—see Chapter 17 (Preventive Maintenance)

Safety/Breakdown Equipment to
Store in Outside Compartments

A *Lidstone Law* of RVing: Regularly check all tires for correct pressure and keep the loaded RV weight under the manufacturer's maximum gross vehicle weight rating (GVWR). The most frequent causes of RV tire failure are underinflation and overloading.

- Spare tire and wheel assemblies for RV, car dolly, and toad (see note 1 below)
- Triangular reflective safety markers (in case of breakdown)
- Battery jumper cables and specific-gravity tester
- Flashlight and batteries
- Wheel chocks
- Spare tire
- Engine oil
- Hydraulic fluid for transmission, slideout, and jacks
- Brake fluid
- 1-gallon water bottle (can be filled from RV fresh water tank) and funnel
- Crank assembly for RV slideout assembly (to retract slideout manually in case of hydraulic failure)
- Heavy-duty duct tape (handy for leaks and temporary repairs)
- Hydraulic or mechanical jack capable of lifting motorhome, recreational trailer, fifth-wheel trailer, loaded car dolly, and toad based on what you are driving and towing (for use if road service is not available or road service does not have an adequate-capacity jack—see note 2 on page 95)

Note 1: RVers should carry spare tire and wheel assemblies inflated to the correct air pressure for the RV, car dolly, and toad. Some RVers don't carry a spare to save space and weight or because there is no storage space provided. They rely on towing services and tire shops to provide whatever they need, which may not be the case and can result in being stranded on the road, trip delays, higher costs for tires or rims, and being unable to get the brand you prefer.

Note 2: Unfortunately, some of the road and towing services may not carry the heavy-duty jacks required for large Class A motorhomes. Therefore, you should consider carrying a jack capable of lifting the RV, even if you have road service.

Hookup Items

Your RV is a home on wheels that provides all the services of a house. Today's motorhomes have internal plumbing with hot and cold water for the kitchen and bath; electric power for lighting, air-conditioning, microwave, TV, and entertainment needs; and cable inputs for the TV and telephone to provide the extensive creature-comforts you want to take on the road.

For short stays, RV users may dry camp, meaning no hookups or just using electricity. For longer stays, sewer, water, electricity, cable TV, and telephone hookups are common.

Hooking up normally only takes a few minutes. The hookup items should be stowed in outside storage bays near the RV utility hookups. A minimum set of hookup items should include:

- Holding tank deodorants and chemicals
- 10 feet of 3-inch-diameter sewer hose with connectors to drain black and gray water holding tanks
- 25 feet of $5/_8$-inch or $1/_2$-inch water hose to supply water to kitchen and bath facilities
- Spray bottle of bathroom/kitchen cleaner, paper towels or old dish towels, and disposable vinyl gloves for tidying up the utility and hookup area
- 25 feet of 30 amp or 50 amp electric hookup cables for 120-volt (AC) power
- 50 feet of coax TV cable
- 5 feet of coax TV cable for wall-mounted bedroom TV

— Voltage meter and/or polarity tester for 120-volt (AC) system (see note below)

Note: Voltage meters ($15–$40) will indicate if the AC power supply (shore power or generator) is providing a low-voltage environment (less than 108 volts) that can damage air-conditioning units, microwave ovens, and some electric appliances. Do not use the 120-volt (AC) shore power provided by the campground or resort if a low-voltage environment exists. Polarity testers (approximately $10) will indicate if the shore power has reversed polarity to create an unsafe electrical condition. Voltage and polarity should be checked when the RV is initially hooked to shore power, and voltage should be checked whenever a potential of low voltage exists (e.g., if you experience dimming lights, etc.). These devices are widely available from hardware stores and RV suppliers in a range of prices.

Although the above hookup supplies and equipment will be adequate for most modern campgrounds, all RVers periodically use older campgrounds that don't have conveniently located hookups. To cover all the bases, we suggest you carry the items listed below on your extended trips:

— Quick-disconnect fitting for all water supply hookups (saves time when hooking up and saves wear and tear on RV water supply/hose fittings)
— Additional 20 feet of 3-inch sewer hose
— Additional sewer connector fittings to enable connecting multiple 10-foot and 20-foot sections
— Additional 25-foot water hose (for a total of 50 feet)
— 25-foot extension power cord to plug into the existing 25-foot power cord (for a total of 50 feet)
— 50 amp–30 amp adapter (in the event the campground does not have 50 amp power)
— 30 amp–20 amp adapter (in the event the campground does not have 30 amp power)
— 50 feet of telephone line and a telephone (you can roll up what you don't need, but you can't stretch it if it's too short)
— Portable 140–300 watt inverter for TV or laptop computer

— Pressure regulator for faucet end of water hose hookup (see note below)

Note: Water pressure regulators protect the RV plumbing from rupturing and any other associated damage caused by excessive water pressure. This is more fully explained in the "Water Hookup" section of Chapter 13 (Setting Up and Taking Down the RV Site).

Recreation and Leisure Items

Additional items to make the trip more enjoyable include:
— RV library—campground directories, travel books, etc.; see Chapter 2 (Trip Planning That Works)
— Music CDs and audiocassettes
— VCR and videocassettes
— Recreational equipment—golf, tennis, swimming, etc.
— Books (paperbacks take up less space and are lighter in weight)
— Small TV for bedroom
— Clock radio
— 120-volt (AC) reading lamp
— Camera and film (see note 1 below)
— Bike rack and bicycles
— Folding chairs
— Picnic cooler and freezer packs
— Tablecloth
— Outside lights
— Citronella candles (see note 2 on page 98)
— Gas grill and propane, or charcoal grill and charcoal (see note 2 on page 98)
— Games—Monopoly, Scrabble, etc.
— Hobby items, such as needlework, knitting, and playing cards
— Extension cords

Note 1: Consider using a digital camera if you are bringing a computer on the trip. You'll be able to view, store, and print your pictures immediately without the need to get rolls of film developed.

Note 2: We recommend butane "gas matches" (costing $3–$8) for lighting candles and grills—and don't forget the remotes and spare batteries for the TVs, VCRs, satellite receiver, stereos, and so forth.

Housekeeping and Miscellaneous Items

— Laundry supplies

— Ice cube trays

— Travel iron and portable ironing board

— Dishes, pots and pans, cutlery

— Kitchen utensils (e.g., can opener, bottle opener, spatulas, etc.)

— Trash bags

— Blankets, sheets, pillowcases, towels, washcloths

— Portable 1,500-watt electric heater (to take off chill without using up propane)

— Paper towels

— Toilet paper

— Suntan lotion and insect repellent

— Cleaning supplies for kitchen and coach interior

— Cleaning supplies, polish, UV protectant, bucket, rags, and lightweight ladder for coach exterior

The RVer should determine which of the items in this category are consistent with personal interests and which of those can be left in the RV. The more supplies and tools stored in the RV permanently, the shorter the loading and unloading time.

CHAPTER 8

CLOSING UP THE HOUSE

RVers enjoy traveling, but it's important to spend a little time securing your home against unintended visitors or damage while you're away. Several key items must be considered when closing up the house. Most people find it takes longer to figure out what to do than it takes to do it. Here's the first pass at a comprehensive list for your use.

The goal of RVers who will be away for a while is to make their homes secure. Therefore, try to avoid making the house look empty while you are away on a trip. We do the same types of things when leaving on an extended RV trip that we do any other time we leave the area for more than a few days.

Home security issues to be considered are related to:

— Household telephone service
— Running the household
— Inside the home
— Outside the home
— While you are gone

What to Do with the Telephone Service

You have several options for dealing with your local household phone service while you're away on extended trips:

— You can leave the phone on with full service if you are going to access an answering machine to check for calls and messages or will call-forward all calls to your cell phone.

— You can have the phone disconnected. However, disconnecting phone service is not recommended because it is unlikely you will be able to get the same phone number when you return. You will also have to pay an installation service charge to restore service upon your return.

— You can check with your local telephone company to see if you can switch to a standby or inactive status that allows you to keep your number with a reduced monthly rate.

"Running the Household" Activities

— Make arrangements for handling the mail—see Chapter 10 (Keeping in Touch).

— Cancel newspaper delivery.

— Cancel garbage and refuse pickup if you pay for service on a monthly basis.

— Cancel or reschedule pest control services.

— Return library books and videotapes.

— Reduce or drop service for satellite and/or cable TV not needed while away.

— If you leave for an extended trip, you will probably designate a house checker (whom we call our "house angel"), who will periodically enter your house to take a look around. Of course, the house checker/angel will need a set of keys. You should discuss and agree upon the procedures to follow if emergency repairs are required, especially if that person may not be able to reach you quickly. Give your house angel the names and phone numbers of any particular home repair contractors you would like called if repairs are needed.

— Show your house angel where all the utility turn-offs are located, including water, electricity, and gas. Putting a large, brightly colored tag or sign on them is fine (it's your house, not theirs).

— Notify law enforcement authorities of the time period that your home will be vacant, and how they can reach you and any designated house checker.

— Notify the alarm or security company of the time period that your home will be vacant, and how they can reach you and any designated house checker. This is important because many security companies call the house phone any time an alarm is activated to verify who is there and confirm an emergency before contacting the fire or police department. If you have a security system wired to the telephone system, the house angel also needs the name and phone number of your alarm company as well as the security code and ID.

- Provide for care of pets remaining at home.
- Provide for care of indoor plants.

Inside the Home

- Leave air-conditioning on and set to 80–82 degrees and leave ceiling fans on low in the summer.
- Leave furnace on and set to 55 degrees in the winter.
- Turn off the faucets for the washing machine.
- Change filters in air cleaners and leave running on low speed.
- Leave closet doors open to reduce possibility of mildew.
- Set timers for lighting circuits (power outages change the start and stop times).
- Turn off the gas or electric supply to the hot water heater.
- Empty refrigerator and set on low setting. If you unplug your refrigerator altogether, you should tape blocks to the doors with masking tape to keep them partially open.
- Pour a little vegetable oil down the inside drain of the dishwasher to keep the diaphragm flexible.
- Pour a little vegetable oil into the garbage disposal to help prevent it from sticking.
- Pour at least a quart of tap water slowly into every drain to fill the plumbing traps (the water in the traps evaporates over time if there is no use).
- Unplug all appliances subject to power surges (e.g., computer equipment, stereos, radios, microwave ovens, sewing machines, etc.).
- Lock all windows and partially close all blinds, shades, curtains, and drapes so that people can't see in but interior lights can be seen from the outside.
- Secure locking bars on all sliding doors and French doors to prevent them from being forced open from outside.
- Turn off power to automatic garage door opener to prevent it from being operated by remote or switch.

- Engage key or mechanical slide latch on garage door and put padlock in hole at the end of the slide latch.
- Lock all doors.
- Activate the alarm or security system.

Outside the Home

- Arrange for snow removal in the winter.
- Dispose of garbage and yard waste if you leave before scheduled pickup.
- Provide for yard, pool, and other outside maintenance tasks as needed in spring, summer, and fall.
- Remove all small, loose items from the exterior of the home that could be blown about by high winds.
- Trim overhanging bushes, trees, and shrubs that are overgrown or may get too large while you're away from home.

While You're Gone

- Leave the utilities (water, gas, and electricity) on. They're required for heating and cooling and may be needed if any repairs or cleaning are done while you are still on the road.
- Have someone (designated angel) check the house in case of adverse weather events and power outages.
- Call the friend, relative, or neighbor checking the house at least once a month to say hello, tell them about the trip, and thank them for their help. Don't ask about the house; they will tell you of any problems anyway.
- Ask your neighbor or house angel to park a car in your driveway from time to time. It helps make your home look occupied.
- Get a gift for the friend, relative, or neighbor checking the house.

Remember that these are just suggested lists. Every RVer has an individual set of needs, so the suggestions provided here are meant to help you in devising your own set of shutdown procedures.

One last item: As you climb into the driver's seat, ask yourself, Are the passengers, wallets, purses, cell phones, checkbook, and credit cards in the RV?

Staying Out on the Road

‒ ‒ ‒ ‒ ‒ ‒

CHAPTER 9

BANKING, MONEY, AND BILL PAYING

RVers should decide in advance how to handle banking, obtaining cash, and paying bills while out on a long trip. Various personal finance options are available to help meet your needs.

Banking and Money

While you're on the road you have two sets of expenses—the regular ones associated with your home base and those related to being away from home. Your concerns while on the road include access to cash, account balances, and transaction activity, as well as the ability to make deposits, transfer funds, and pay bills.

RVers' personal finance options and needs include:

‒ Cash and bank accounts
‒ Overdraft protection
‒ ATM and debit cards
‒ Credit cards

You have advantages of overdraft protection and ATM and debit cards along with bank accounts and credit cards to help handle your banking and expense needs. Overdraft protection keeps checks from bouncing. ATM and debit cards are linked to your checking or savings account and make it easy to obtain needed cash and avoid writing checks.

Cash and Bank Accounts

Your first option is to bring enough cash or traveler's checks to meet all your anticipated expenses with the ability to replenish the cash supply for unanticipated needs. If you use traveler's checks, many credit unions and local banks offer them to customers at no charge.

Your second option is to use regular banking via a checking account and an ATM/debit card. You should consider using a regional or national bank with offices and branches in all or most of the areas you are driving through or visiting. This option enables RVers to reduce or eliminate ATM charges and to have access to bank services, account balances, and transaction activity. Many banks offer reduced-fee or no-fee accounts for retirees; provide internet access to your bank account activity; and offer automated bill-paying services. Consult with your bank to determine the best terms and conditions for you.

Another option for banking is an internet-banking checking account and an ATM/debit card. You should ensure that your internet bank will provide ATM/debit card access, and a rebate or allowance of ATM user fees (when charged) in all or most of the areas you are driving through or visiting to reduce or eliminate ATM charges. As with regular checking accounts at local, regional, or national banks, you should consider using electronic funds transfer (EFT), described below, for all paycheck or retirement check deposits.

Many internet banks have minimal to no fees, pay interest on accounts, and pay rebates on debit card transactions. So instead of paying a monthly service fee, you receive interest and rebates. Also, you have internet access to your bank account activity, the ability to transfer money between accounts at the bank, and the benefit of automated bill-paying services.

We strongly recommend that you use electronic funds transfer to deposit all periodic checks (paychecks, retirement checks, dividends, etc.) into your bank accounts. All state and federal agencies and many business and financial organizations prefer you to use EFT. Advantages of EFT deposits include safety and the convenience of having the funds deposited to your accounts the evening before the due date. This makes the money available from ATM machines, debit card transactions, and checks on the day they are due, whereas many banks place holds on deposited paychecks to allow for clearance.

Don't forget to update your checkbook register to reflect these payments. EFT deposits may be shown on your bank statements as "ACH CREDIT" with the name of the payer beside it.

Obviously, we recommend that you use a ATM/debit card from a regional, national, or internet bank to meet all your cash needs. Look for low fees, widespread and free ATM/debit card access, and access to account transaction activity.

Overdraft Protection

Overdraft protection equals peace of mind while traveling because this service keeps checks from "bouncing" due to insufficient funds. Your financial viability is protected and you have continued availability of funds until you take any necessary corrective action.

Most banks tie a bank-issued Visa or MasterCard number to your checking account. They may also offer the option of transferring from another account at the bank or setting up an automatic overdraft loan. They will transfer funds up to the limit of the credit card, overdraft agreement, or balance of the transferred-from account.

Be sure to check with your bank regarding all expenses associated with overdraft protection. The most advantageous plans have no monthly fee, transaction fee, or transfer fee and only charge interest from the date of transfer. If your bank does charge fees, consider finding a new bank.

We advise you to make arrangements with your bank for overdraft protection, but remind you also to take all necessary precautions regarding lost checks and ATM/debit cards. Notify the bank immediately if this occurs. Otherwise, the bank will continue to transfer funds to your account while a non-authorized person might be using the lost checks or ATM/debit card.

ATM and Debit Cards

ATM cards are used at ATM machines to check bank balances and make cash withdrawals from your checking account. They require a PIN (personal identification number) to execute a transaction. Protect your PIN information, and do not keep the PIN in the wallet or pocket book with the ATM card.

Debit card transactions are executed directly against your checking account, generally showing up no later than the end of the next business day. Debit card transactions will be shown on your monthly checking account statement. Most debit cards include an ATM capability and a cash-back capability. There is no charge when you use the cash-back feature, but you will need to remember to use the PIN. The cash-back feature allows you to obtain additional cash back when you make a sales transaction using your debit card. The amount varies and can be anywhere from $20 to $100 depending on the store. The cash-back feature may save you some trips to the ATM.

As with ATM cards, you must protect your PIN information. Keep in mind that any one who obtains your debit card and also knows the PIN can empty your bank account. *Again, do not keep the PIN in the wallet or pocket book with the debit card.*

A debit card can also be used as a charge card wherever major credit cards are accepted. When used as a charge card, because it has either a Visa or MasterCard logo, you will need to sign the credit card slip in lieu of entering the PIN. The withdrawal will still be deducted from your checking account, however.

We recommend you carry credit cards as backup in case of possible problems with debit cards. We've run into minor problems in some areas in the Northeast trying to get cash back at supermarkets. We didn't understand the reason, as the card worked with no problems at the local bank and credit union ATMs in the same area. Don't panic if this occurs; the problem is invariably the network connection at the store, not your card.

As with EFT deposits, don't forget to enter all ATM and debit card transactions in your checkbook register.

Credit Cards

Credit cards allow you to travel without carrying large amounts of cash. They also give you the benefit of a written record of expenses by receipt and on the monthly statement. Use of credit cards lets you charge expenses and pay for them later. Everyone knows that credit cards are simply deferred bills that eventually must be paid. Although credit cards make it easy to spend too much money, you can stay on budget by considering in advance the types of items or services you may need to buy (or will be tempted to purchase) while traveling. You can then calculate the approximate cost of such items, set a limit on charged amounts, and avoid surprises (and panic attacks) when the bill arrives.

Your credit card can be used to get cash advances at any banks displaying the logo on your credit card. The banks generally display the logos of the credit systems they honor (e.g., Visa, MasterCard, etc.). We recommend that you only use credit cards for cash advances in the event of emergencies when other options such as your ATM or debit card are not available. The extra service fees, which may be based on the amount of the cash advance, as well as interest charges higher than the regular rate for purchases, start accruing the day you receive the cash advance and add up very quickly.

You can also use a credit card for cash advances from most ATMs rather than having to go into a bank. Advances from ATMs require a PIN and their size may be limited. Contact the credit card issuer for a PIN if one was not issued with the card. And again, in our experience, it's easier to get a cash advance from a bank or credit union ATM than from a supermarket ATM. We don't understand the reason for this discrepancy, but it seems to exist.

It is important to keep a list of the debit, ATM, and credit card account numbers and associated telephone numbers in a place separate from the cards, in case of loss, theft, or other problems.

Paying Bills

There are at least five ways to pay bills:
- Write up your checks before you leave and bring them with you.
- Have a neighbor or relative pay for you.
- Pay by check while on the road.
- Pay with the automated bill-paying feature of your checking account.
- Pay via EFT, credit card, or debit card.

Using the Checkbook

Writing up your checks before you leave and taking them with you works fine if you're only going to be away from home for less than four to six weeks. We recommend mailing on the road because bank, mortgage, and car payments may be credited (in total) to the current month and principal if you pay them in advance. They may then hit you with missing/late-payment notices and fees for the successive months. Utilities can be prepaid because excess payment amounts become a credit balance that rolls forward to the next billing period.

Having a neighbor or relative send in payments can also help. If they collect or receive your mail, they can pay your bills. The disadvantage is that you will have to leave blank, presigned checks and you may not know what your real balance is without contacting them to merge your check, ATM, and debit transactions with the checks they write.

Even if you have your mail forwarded, bills may arrive too late to be paid on time. If you are in the situation in which your mail has caught up to you and you believe time is sufficient, use your statements as usual. Otherwise, you can simply pay your fixed bills (e.g., mortgage, cable, car loan, etc.) as usual because you know the amount due. For your remaining bills, you can estimate or deliberately overpay the anticipated amounts due, or contact the creditors using their toll-free numbers to obtain the current balances.

To pay by check while on the road, when you don't have the actual bill or statement, you need to have a list of pertinent information that includes payee addresses and phone numbers, amounts to be paid, and account numbers. You will also need the typical supplies of envelopes, stamps, index cards, and checkbook. Simply pay the bill as you would normally, but use an index card in place of your usual statement stub. It should include your name, address, account number, and the amount you have enclosed.

The other option, if you are the incredibly organized sort of person, is to preprint labels on your computer. One row would have your return address, one row would have the payee addresses, and the last row would have the same information you would normally write on the index card. With this method you need just slap the information label on an index card, slap the address labels on the envelope along with a stamp, enclose the check, and mail that sucker off.

If you are especially computer savvy, you might also consider preprinting envelopes to cut out the expense of buying labels. This simply requires feeding the envelopes through your computer printer. Rubber return-address stamps also come in very handy for expediting the bill-paying process.

Automated Bill Paying

Automated bill paying can be set up with your bank. Banks generally offer two options:

- Telephone-accessible services that allow you to instruct a bank representative to pay bills for you
- Using banking software and a computer or personal digital assistant (PDA) with access to the internet

Both options allow you to create a set of fixed payments to be paid with no other action required of you while traveling. These two bill-paying options also give you the ability to contact the bank by telephone or by using a PC or PDA to delete or modify existing payments on-line. The same methods can be used to create new payments that will be processed periodically or on a one-time basis. Both of these methods are very effective and easy to use.

The use of PCs and PDAs is covered in Chapter 10 (Keeping in Touch). If you want to modify your transactions or control release of payments on the road with your computer or PDA, you will need access to a personal or laptop computer or PDA, phone line access or cellular modem access, and banking software with a bill-paying feature. The automated bill-paying features supported by the bank include any necessary additional software required on your computer and may provide the capability to update personal financial management applications such as Quicken or Money installed on your computer or PDA.

EFT, Debit Card, and Credit Card Payments

EFT and debit card transactions are processed directly against your checking account, much the same as regular checks. Credit card payments are added to your credit card balance and interest accrues on the amount from the day it is posted on the credit card balance. Some creditors will accept the payment information over the phone to start, modify, or stop payment methods; the rest will require completion of printed forms.

A number of creditors, including most home mortgage processors, will be glad to use your checking account number to process an EFT transaction against your account. A limited number of businesses will accept your credit card number or debit card number for payment, although any creditor who accepts payments by credit card can also process payments by debit card (as long as it has a Visa or MasterCard logo). If your creditor is using your debit card or credit card number, keep in mind that the creditor will also need the expiration date. When your cards are renewed, be sure to give the new date to the creditors or the payment requests will be rejected. Most banks will not accept credit cards for payment on Visa or MasterCard accounts, but some, including Discover, will accept payment by debit card.

CHAPTER 10

KEEPING IN TOUCH

Keeping in touch with friends, relatives, and colleagues will help you stay up-to-date on their needs and activities, and will allow you to share your recent experiences with those closest to you. In this chapter you will learn about the options available to you for keeping in touch over the phone and through the mail, including how to handle your mail while traveling and how to use the internet for your written communications.

On the Phone

Keeping in touch verbally is a high priority for most RVers. Readily available options include:

- Cellular phones
- Two-way pagers
- Regular phones
- Answering machines/services
- Pay phones
- Prepaid long distance calling cards
- Long distance calling cards
- Satellite telephones

Cellular Phones

Cellular phones offer the most convenience to RVers. They can operate in analog, digital, or dual (both) modes. It is recommended that you use a cell phone with dual capability and a service plan that does not charge extra for long distance calls. Digital phones can provide voicemail, caller ID, and messaging capabilities. It is imperative to compare the various plans.

First of all, determine your own service needs. Would you like a short- or long-term contract? What penalty would you be willing to pay (if any) to cancel service at any time? What do you consider to be acceptable fees for connecting and disconnecting service? How many minutes do you need per billing period?

If you are interested in unlimited long distance capability, choose a service that does not charge extra for long distance calls made from outside your local area. Some cellular services include free long distance for calls originated within the local billing/service area, but charge extra if you are outside that area longer than a specific period.

Sprint PCS, AT&T, Alltel, Nextel, and Verizon are popular because they offer wide services areas, features, and coverage with the least restrictions, but you should compare all plans aggressively because the wireless industry is continuously bringing out new providers, products, options, and pricing structures. Make sure that your coverage meets both your needs at home and those out on the road.

Because of the recent major drop in per-minute charges, many RVers are electing to carry two cell phones when they travel, allowing a couple to keep in easy contact when one is away from the RV. If you are considering this option, you may want to consider the plans that allow you to share minutes between two phones. We've been very happy with Sprint PCS because it provides free long distance in the areas we visit and we share the total minutes between two phones for an additional fee of $20 a month, which is cheaper than any of the other plans we looked at. Because the rates and availability for this feature vary by provider, you have to check to see which carriers best meet your needs.

If you will be carrying a cell phone that stores phone numbers on your trips, we strongly recommend you store the following phone numbers and names in the phone:

- Medical providers including doctors, dentists, pharmacy, insurance, and HMOs
- Emergency and road service
- Friends or relatives to contact in an emergency
- RV service facilities you plan on using
- Campgrounds and resorts you plan to visit

This gives you the ability to contact people quickly in the event of emergencies, make or modify dates and arrival times for reservations or RV service, or request information while you're on the road or away from the RV. You can delete the campground and resort numbers when you no longer need them.

Two-Way Pagers

Two-way pagers provide a way to keep in touch but have limitations in terms of cost and coverage areas. These devices use wireless technology to display messages and e-mail, as well as news, weather, and sports information. In addition, they may also offer voicemail and automatic bill-paying service. Although these multifunctional products were designed for business and commercial use, they are also useful for casual and recreational activities.

Two-way pagers cost approximately $80–$100 to purchase, and have a monthly access fee starting at approximately $20. Providers may offer a generous rebate if you sign a twelve-month service agreement. We suggest you verify that two-way pager service is available in all the geographic areas you will be visiting, because there are large areas where pagers cannot be reached. You cannot send any outgoing messages or receive any incoming messages when you are outside a pager service area. Incoming messages will be saved until you get back into an area with service. Your pager will beep when you enter a service area and it begins receiving an adequate signal.

Providers are continuously introducing new two-way pager services. The major drawback of using a two-way pager is that monthly access charges can soar for extensive use (as compared to the costs of other methods of communicating).

Regular Phones

Consider putting a telephone jack in your RV and bringing along a regular or portable telephone and a 50-foot cable. Quite a few RV resorts and campgrounds will arrange for telephone line installation by the local phone company. Also, more and more campgrounds and RV resorts provide selected RV sites that include telephone line jacks along with electricity and cable TV.

Some campgrounds such as the Ocean Lakes Family Campground in Myrtle Beach, South Carolina, offer free telephone service for local calls and modem hookups at the campsite. Others will charge a low daily rate for local calls. Generally, campgrounds and resorts providing free or low-cost phone hookups at the individual sites require you to use a long distance calling card (see below) for long distance calls.

Answering Machines/Services

To accept calls at your home base after you leave on a trip and the house is closed up, you can use either an answering machine or sign up for local telephone company–provided voicemail. With an answering machine, you can call your own phone and enter a code to listen to messages. The local phone company's voicemail service provides an access phone number and a PIN that allows you to retrieve voicemail messages while you're on the road.

If you use an answering machine, make sure it has a toll-saver function that alerts you when there are messages pending by beeping before it switches over to the message processing function. The tone and number of beeps may vary, depending upon the manufacturer and model. This allows you to disconnect the call before it is completed to avoid having to pay for the call when you know there are no new messages.

Another option to the answering machine or voicemail on your home phone is to use one of the free services that provide free message, fax, and e-mail services over the phone. This is explained in the "E-mail and Internet Access via Telephone" section further on in this chapter.

Pay Phones

Pay phones represent the old-school approach to calling home. You can use them by inserting money, credit cards, or long distance calling cards. We recommend using coins to place local calls, but calling cards are more economical for long distance.

Prepaid Long Distance Calling Cards

Prepaid calling cards are sold with a given amount of minutes or units of long distance service. (When you have used all the minutes, simply dispose of the card.) They are generally quite inexpensive and are available from most of the RV user groups or from the cashier in local supermarkets, convenience stores, office supply stores, and discount stores.

It is important for RVers to ensure that any prepaid card purchased will work from your destination and the locations along the way. These cards can be found with rates as low as four cents per minute (e.g., 500-minute AT&T cards available at Sam's Warehouse), and possibly lower. The cards come with a wide variety of total minutes, units, and costs per minute and expiration dates. When used from a pay phone, an additional charge of twenty-nine cents per call is charged for use of the provider's toll-free access number over and above the per-minute charges. You should always check a prepaid card's rates and other factors to determine if a long distance calling card is a better option.

Long Distance Calling Cards

Long distance calling cards are available from your local telephone service provider, your long distance provider for your home telephone, and most of the RV user groups. Good Sam offers very low per-minute charges for their members. Generally, long distance calling cards require you to dial a toll-free number from any telephone, including pay phones. An instruction menu usually will ask you to enter the number you are calling, your home telephone number, and a four-digit PIN. As with prepaid long distance cards, these cards also incur an additional charge of twenty-nine cents per call for use of the provider's toll-free access number over and above the per-minute charges when used from a pay phone.

Consider traveling with a low-cost-per-minute calling card even if you have a good cellular plan with free long distance. That way, if you wind up in a roaming area or cannot get cellular reception, you will have a backup for low-cost long distance service.

You need to compare different plans to see who is offering the best rates. The long distance calling cards are substantially cheaper than the pay-phone rates for long distance calls. Don't assume, however, that your local and long distance telephone providers always have the best rates. For instance, our home phone's long distance rate is five cents a minute with no monthly fee, but the same long distance provider's calling card rate is about fifty cents a minute.

Satellite Telephones

If none of the above works for you and money is no object, there is the James Bond approach. The satellite phone, costing about $3,000, fits in a case about the size of a laptop computer. You can use it to make calls to and receive calls from people anywhere in the world. Satellite phones are normally used by people at sea or those who travel to really remote places. Satellite phones are available with a number of accessories and features including encryption, fax, and data communications that increase the price substantially. Airtime for calls is purchased in prepaid blocks of time (usually a $250 minimum) and costs about $3 per minute for connect time. RVers interested in obtaining additional information about this type of product should check out the Magellan satellite accessories website at www.magellangps.com for more information.

In Writing

Keeping in written touch is also important for most RVers. You can either send "snail mail" through the U.S. Postal Service or send e-mail messages via the internet. The overnight delivery services (e.g., FedEx, Airborne, Express Mail, etc.) can get paper-based mail delivered fastest when time is of the essence.

Handling the Mail

You can use any or all of the methods listed below to handle mail while away from home. If you can think of some others (perhaps carrier pigeons?), go for it!

- Let it pile up on your doorstep (not recommended at all).
- Have a neighbor or relative pick it up.
- Start mail hold by the U.S. Postal Service (USPS).
- Start mail forwarding by the USPS.
- Start mail hold/forwarding by a private mail service.

The USPS will hold your mail for periods of thirty days or less. Short forms are available at every post office to inform the USPS of the start and stop dates for your particular hold period. If you find you have to change the information while on the road, you can stop in a post office anywhere, submit a new form, and have the hold time modified.

In addition to visiting the post office, you can reach the USPS by phone at 1-800-275-8777 to establish a mail hold (in most locations) and obtain phone numbers and addresses of post offices. You can also access the USPS website on the internet at www.usps.com for the following types of information and activities:

— Print out blank change-of-address forms. You have to complete, sign, and give the form to your carrier or mail it to the post office that delivers your mail.

— Locate the address and phone number of any post office.

— Provide information on how to notify mailers of your new address (if mail is to be forwarded).

— Link to the Mapquest.com website to obtain maps, driving directions, and trip planning.

The USPS is continually upgrading service offerings nationwide. We recommend you contact them to confirm the USPS phone and internet services available at the time of your departure on an extended trip.

If your trip is extended beyond thirty days, you can get around the USPS's thirty-day limit by using a procedure that we have found to be successful. A few days before the initial thirty-day hold period ends, go to a post office and submit a follow-up form that shows a start date that is identical to the end date of the current form on file. By following this procedure, the USPS will accommodate you for a "follow-on" period.

If you plan to be gone more than thirty days, you should extend to your postal carrier the courtesy of telling them that you will be going away. Most carriers will go out of their way to explain your options to you and to assist in any way they can.

Mail forwarding by the USPS is fine for trips of up to one year from the start date. Your first-class, priority, and express mail will be forwarded for twelve months; magazines and periodicals will be forwarded for two months; and junk mail will be destroyed. The USPS provides a short form listing your home address, forwarding address, start date, and end date. The form can be completed at the post office or mailed to any post office. Officially, the USPS says forwarding information is activated within twenty-four hours. If time is of the essence, the USPS recommends turning in the mail forwarding request directly to your current post office rather than giving it to your carrier or mailing it to your post office to minimize delays in starting up the forwarding activity. We recommend that you plan for a three-day delay before mail forwarding begins. For instance, if you are leaving on a Monday, list the previous Thursday as your start date.

Because the USPS charges nothing to hold and forward your mail, and because the service can be started, stopped, or changed at any post office, we recommend using the USPS. We have always found the USPS personnel at post offices around the country, and the personnel contacted via the 800 telephone number, to be very helpful when we've had to change our mail hold and forwarding instructions due to changes in our trip itinerary. Many RVers use mail forwarding service until about two weeks before returning home. At that time, they cancel the forwarding and start a mail hold. This strategy permits all the forwarded mail to be flushed out of the forwarding system before the RVer gets home.

Mail hold/forwarding by private mail services is also fine for trips of any duration. There are a number of excellent services available from the major RV user groups, and many other services can be found through their advertisements in the various RV magazines. They generally provide at least a mail hold/forwarding service and a message service for friends or relatives trying to get in contact with the RVer. Most have toll-free numbers for customers. The advantage of the private companies is that they have a broader range of services to offer. For instance, the private mail service may provide a twenty-four-hour emergency phone number that friends, relatives, and colleagues can call if they want to reach you. The service will then attempt to contact you. Because prices and service offerings vary, be sure to comparison shop to determine the best options for your needs.

Both the USPS and the private mail services protect the integrity of your mail and offer excellent service and security. Your decision between the two should be based strictly on personal preference and convenience.

On the Internet

The internet provides RVers with the wonderful advantage of electronic mail (e-mail), which is an inimitably convenient, speedy, and reliable way to communicate globally with others. More and more RVers are opting to use the internet to keep in contact with friends and relatives via e-mail and to access the thousands of websites and chat rooms that are available. Numerous providers support the RVer's e-mail needs either at no cost or for a minimal fee.

Internet access is possible through a variety of e-mail–enabled devices and computers. There is definitely an affordable device suitable for every RVer's needs. All the equipment we describe can be obtained from electronics, discount, and office supply stores, including Best Buy, Circuit City, Office Depot, OfficeMax, and RadioShack. E-mail–ready devices can also be purchased over the internet. Have fun shopping around and trying out these fantastic communication devices, because you will surely find a model that fits your budget, be it large or small (either the device or the budget!).

The various options available to the RVer who wants to send and receive e-mail using the internet are, in ascending order of cost:

- E-mail and internet access via telephone
- Internet-ready cellular phones
- E-mail appliances
- Internet appliances
- Personal digital assistants (PDAs) with internet or wireless capability
- Global satellite communicators
- Laptop or PC computers and modem

E-mail and Internet Access Via Telephone

Recently, an amazing new free telephone e-mail service became available to anyone with access to any type of phone—regular, cellular, or pay phone. No computer or electronic device other than a phone is needed to set up an account and to have access to the following offerings:

- Receive voicemail messages
- Send outgoing voicemail messages to other e-mail accounts
- Receive faxes
- Receive text-based e-mail converted to audio for listening to on the phone

Although this may sound unbelievable, it is true. These telephone-enabled voice portal e-mail services are a boon to us all and are very easy to use. The services were developed to provide another method of access for business people and travelers, and the number of providers is increasing as the demand for and use of these features and services grow.

Although they are available on both a free and a fee basis (monthly charges apply), the fee-based services primarily directed at business may provide more extensive features. Two current providers that may be of use to RVers include Onebox.com (free) and uReach.com (combination of free and low-fee offerings).

The person wishing to send and receive e-mail over the phone can set up an account by telephone or by linking to the free e-mail service's site on a computer; the second option is faster, however. Simply follow the instructions provided to create a voice portal internet account for access to e-mail, instant messaging, and other personal information. You will be asked to provide two sets of identifiers:

- User name and password for use when logged onto the internet
- Numeric PIN or password for accessing your account on the phone

The RVer is given a phone number and extension to contact the service, and an e-mail account is opened at the voice portal website under the RVer's user name. People can leave voicemail messages for you or send faxes by dialing the assigned phone number and following the instructions. They send e-mail to the user name on the e-mail account you have established.

We recommend you check out the internet sites for Onebox.com and uReach.com to determine which seems appropriate for your needs. Both services provide free voicemail service. As indicated above, Onebox.com provides all their services at no cost; uReach.com provides the same types of services plus discounted long distance services, all at reasonable rates.

In summary, these new systems use text-voice synthesis technology to convert text-based e-mail to an audio message. RVers can receive voicemail messages and faxes, retrieve e-mail messages, and send voice replies to other e-mail accounts by phone. You can also check, receive, and send e-mail messages by any other device that can access the internet.

The free voice portal systems for checking e-mail, voicemail messages, and incoming faxes are very helpful to RVers on extended trips. We recommend that you use these services in addition to the basic e-mail service provided by your regular internet service provider (ISP), such as CompuServe, AOL, or other ISPs. We ask our friends, relatives, and associates to send e-mail to our IDs on both the regular e-mail account and our voice portal account accessed by phone (they just enter both IDs on the "To" block of the message). This allows us to use the phone when we don't have access to a telephone line for the PC.

In addition to the two providers discussed above, AOL also offers AOL by Phone for an additional $4.95 per month to their members. It works with any phone by calling an 800 number and provides e-mail, news, stock prices, and other services. Check with AOL for the latest features, availability, access information, and costs.

Again, as demand for this type of service grows, other providers may begin offering similar services on a free or fee basis. Check out available providers and select the one that best meets your RVing and travel needs in terms of ease of use, flexibility, features, and costs.

Internet-ready Cellular Telephones ($50–$300)

Several of the major cellular services provide internet access via digital cellular phones. Their cell phones are capable of accessing the internet for e-mail messages and selected internet services. Certain cell phones can also be used to connect a laptop computer or PC to the internet. It is important to review the accessories required, the availability of service, and the total cost when shopping around for cellular access to e-mail or internet services.

Internet-ready cell phones start as low as $50 and generally cost no more than $300. If your current phone is not internet-ready, you will have to purchase a new phone with the desired features. In addition to the phone, most cell phone providers charge an additional monthly fee of approximately $10 for internet access. The time you are connected to the internet counts against the contracted minutes of your plan.

E-mail Appliances ($50–$180)

Everyone likes access to e-mail, but what if you don't have a computer or find it inconvenient to bring one on a trip? It's now possible to send and receive e-mail without using a computer by using an e-mail appliance. These products connect to your e-mail provider, and automatically send your outgoing messages and receive your incoming messages. E-mail appliances are small, light, inexpensive products that consist of a display and keyboard; they are easy and fun to use. There are also e-mail appliances that work with a personal digital assistant (PDA) but that do not have a keyboard (although you may be able to purchase a miniature plug-in keyboard for the PDA). In addition to the cost of an e-mail appliance, e-mail providers charge a monthly fee of approximately $10. An important feature of these devices is the capability to read and write messages off-line, while not connected, or on-line while connected. This allows you to create and read messages at your leisure without feeling rushed or tying up phone lines.

There are also a number of two-way pagers that can be used for e-mail. The advantages of pagers include their small size, automatic receipt and storage of incoming messages, which can be displayed at your convenience, and message forwarding capability (messages can be sent to other phones or e-mail addressees). They are also popular because they don't require access to a telephone or telephone jack. The drawbacks of pagers for RVers are the lack of coverage in some geographic areas and higher monthly service fees compared to other e-mail appliances.

There are two types of e-mail appliances. The first type of e-mail appliance is a plug-in device (costing approximately $80–$100) that plugs into a telephone jack to connect with the e-mail provider to receive and transmit e-mail messages. These products have monthly service fees of approximately $10 for nationwide toll-free telephone access. Manufacturers of products requiring a connection to a telephone jack include:

— Cidco MailStation

— Vtech e-Mail PostBox

— Landel LT-301 MailBug

To send and receive e-mail with the above products, simply type the message into the device via the keyboard. When you are ready to send, connect the device to the telephone jack and dial the provider's toll-free number. The e-mail appliance will connect to the provider and automatically send your outgoing messages and receive your incoming messages. You then end the call and unplug from the telephone system. You can read the messages at any time. Most of the e-mail appliances can store several hundred messages.

The second type of e-mail appliance is slightly more expensive, costing approximately $100–$120. It does not require a phone line or phone jack, but instead uses a built-in acoustic coupler to transfer data between the device and the telephone. Sending and receiving e-mail is similar to the process described above, except you hold the e-mail appliance close to the handset part of any telephone instead of plugging it into a telephone jack. The acoustic couplers work with any type of phone, including pay phones, cellular phones, PBX, or regular phones.

The PocketMail e-mail appliance is an example of the acoustic coupler type that does not require connecting to an actual telephone line. These devices operate on batteries and are available with a PC link cable and other accessories. The monthly service charge for PocketMail devices for nationwide toll-free telephone access is approximately $12–$15. There are several models available, including one that works with selected PDAs using the Palm operating system.

PocketMail devices can also be purchased over the internet or may be available from selected Office Depot, Staples, and OfficeMax stores. The internet site for information is www.pocketmail.com.

Both the plug-in and acoustic types of e-mail products provide excellent e-mail service. In terms of picking one, you have to look into and consider your individual needs and the product capabilities (e.g., screen and keyboard size, need for telephone jack, message storage capacity, etc.). Before making a purchase, verify that the access method (plug-in or acoustic coupler) of your chosen device is satisfactory for your specific destinations.

Unless all or most of your destination campgrounds and resorts provide telephone jacks at the RV site, we recommend choosing a device that uses an acoustic coupler. The acoustic coupler–based e-mail appliance provides the most flexibility in reaching e-mail providers and is easy to use and reasonably priced.

Internet Appliances ($300–$600)

An internet appliance, which can also be called a Web or information appliance, is about the size of a small laptop. It is equipped with an LCD display, keyboard, multiple phone jacks, and a built-in modem. Internet appliances require monthly service charges of about $20–$25, access to a wired telephone line (cannot operate with a cellular phone), and 120-volt (AC) power. They provide access to both personal e-mail and all internet sites, and sometimes provide one or more universal serial bus (USB) ports and a printer port. The more expensive ones are compatible with a PDA and include some built-in software applications, such as scheduling.

The higher-end internet appliances are an excellent choice if you want access to your e-mail and to the internet (for news, shopping, trip routing, etc.), but don't need or want a computer. They can be obtained from consumer electronics stores, office supply stores, and over the internet.

Manufacturers and their devices include:
— Cidco Mivo 300 Series Web and e-mail appliance
— WebTV (requires special satellite dish and receiver)

- 3Com Audrey Web Appliance
- Compaq iPAQ Appliance (available in two models)

Factors to Consider in Selecting E-mail or Internet Appliances

Because all the internet- and e-mail–enabled devices are very convenient and easy to use, they can be very helpful while on the road. In making your selection, you might want to get answers to the following questions:

- What is the cost of the appliance?
- Is the device easy to use?
- What is the monthly, quarterly, or annual fee?
- Are specific service providers required? If so, are they available to you?
- Can/will you use the device at home?
- Can service be stopped or started without activation/setup fees or penalties?
- What is the minimum sign-up period for service?
- Are there any limits on number or length of messages?
- Can the device receive faxes?
- Does the e-mail or internet appliance require access to a telephone line or telephone jack?
- Can you use any telephone (i.e., cellular phone, pay phone, or regular telephone) to connect?
- Does the e-mail appliance work with a cellular phone or PDA?
- Can the provider gain access to or route messages from other e-mail accounts?
- Can the appliance be connected to a printer to print out messages?
- Does the device have an address book function?
- How many messages can the device store?

Personal Digital Assistants ($450–$800)

PDAs are small, compact personal organizers that provide scheduling, address book, and task list capabilities. The two popular technologies are the Palm Pilot series, which uses the Palm operating system, and the Pocket PC devices, which use Microsoft software.

Palm Pilots and Pocket PCs can be used both to send and receive e-mail messages and to wirelessly link to the internet using features similar to those of cellular phones.

The devices also run a variety of specialized software applications and have a price range of $249–$499, depending on the model. In addition to the offerings of Palm Pilot and Pocket PC devices, Sony and Handspring offer PDA products that use the Palm operating system. For RVers who like the Palm Pilot devices and cellular phones, Sprint PCS has a combination PCS phone and Palm Pilot. The unit supports all Palm Pilot functions, cell phone functions, e-mail, and access to the internet.

The Pocket PC technology enables PDAs to store entire books in e-book (electronic book) format and to operate as an MP3 music player. Current manufacturers of PDAs with Pocket PC technology include Hewlett-Packard and Compaq.

To send and receive e-mail or connect to the internet on a PDA, you will need some accessories and computer software that can add considerably to the total cost of the PDA. Accessories and niceties you may want or need include cable kit, leather case, keyboard, extra memory, stylus, and battery charger. You can also link a PDA to your desktop or laptop PC to synchronize files and e-mail. Some PDAs can also connect to e-mail appliances.

Internet services for PDAs are available from a number of providers with rates starting at approximately $10 per month. Expanded coverage can cost $25–$50 per month. Make sure that the PDA of your choice meets your needs and that PDA internet service is available in your destination areas.

Global Satellite Communicators ($1,000)

In addition to the e-mail appliances that cost about $100 and the PDAs that cost $250 and up, there is one other type of e-mail appliance called a global satellite communicator. As the name implies, these devices provide world-wide availability to send and receive your e-mail by bouncing it off satellites from anywhere on the globe. Global satellite communication devices, such as the Magellan GSC 100, are very impressive-looking, with features and prices to match. The devices cost approximately $1,000, and you can double that with accessories and add-ons. These devices are for people far away from everything and for whom cost is not an issue.

Features available include navigation and location information using global positioning satellite (GPS) technology, and sending and receiving e-mail and text messages. The minimum monthly fee for service is about $30, with limits on the number and length of messages allowed before incurring additional charges. RVers interested in obtaining additional information about this type of product should check out the Magellan website at www. magellangps.com for more information.

Laptop or Desktop Computer ($600–$1,500)

A laptop or personal computer with a modem can send and receive e-mail through any wired telephone line or internet-ready cellular phone connection. Laptop computers are available for approximately $1,000 and up. Desktop computers are less expensive, costing approximately $600 and up. Both types of computer usually come with an operating system (generally Windows or Macintosh), some limited applications programs, and a modem. Be prepared to install additional computer programs for your individual needs, including mapping and routing software, for use on the road.

Many campgrounds are becoming "modem-friendly" by providing telephone line access for RVers at their individual sites; check the major campground directories to determine which are modem-friendly. The "RVs, Computers, and the Internet" section of Chapter 2 (Trip Planning That Works) discusses the resources and requirements to access the internet using your laptop or personal computer.

Technology Wrap-Up

Disclaimer

The primary purpose of RVing is recreation. We give you this information about technological products merely to let you know what's available, not to set you adrift in a sea of technojargon. None of these gadgets is required for you to thoroughly enjoy your travels.

When considering the use of electronic gadgets, you can assess your own wants and needs by determining the amount and type of information you anticipate using when on extended trips. You also must consider your own comfort level with the services, devices, hardware, and software available. You can then either start shopping for gadgets or ignore them altogether to become as disconnected as possible from all modern communication methods (which is not uncommon among RVers).

In Summary

— Most RVers find that using the USPS for holding or forwarding mail is a great idea. RVers also effectively and conveniently use long distance calling cards and prepaid calling cards for their telephone needs.

— Digital cell phones are recommended because of their ease of use, expanded service offerings (such as internet access), and the attractive price reductions that have become available in the last year or two (such as free long distance, voicemail, and low cost-per-minute charges). They also offer a little extra peace of mind because they ensure that help is only a convenient phone call away.

— The purchase and monthly fees for e-mail and internet appliances are reasonable, but most e-mail–enabled devices require a wired phone line connection.

— If you currently own and use a PDA or computer, consider bringing it along on your RV trips, especially if you have the software and accessories for trip routing or GPS, or a cell phone that can provide your computer with internet access.

CHAPTER 11

DRIVING

Don't count on getting any driving tips from the RV dealer or salesperson. You get more instructions from a salesperson when you buy a microwave or a VCR. However, you can learn how to make driving your RV easier and safer, and we will help you do so. In this chapter, we share our personal experience and some very helpful comments and suggestions from other RVers, RV user publications, and RV service shops.

Whenever you stop—for gas, meals, rest, whatever—take five minutes to walk all around the RV (and toad) and check that:

- Toad connections, including electrical and air hose connections, are not loose
- Safety chains are not loose
- Tires are not running too hot
- Awning clamps are in place
- All compartment doors are closed and tight
- Bicycle and bike racks are properly secured
- Nothing else is loose, dangling, or out of place

This is also a good time to clean the side mirrors and windshield if required and check tire air pressure.

Driving Tips

- Plan on an actual driving time of approximately five to six hours a day plus stops. This schedule allows you to get on the road by 9:00 A.M. without being rushed and to be in a campground by about 4:00 P.M.
- Your RV requires a much longer stopping distance and stopping time than an automobile. Vehicles in tow, especially those without a braking system, increase the time and distance it takes to stop or slow down even more. Be sure to allow for adequate distance and time to stop or slow

down for exits, traffic intersections or lane changes, and vehicles in front of you.

— Remember that while overhead clearance on the Interstate Highway System is normally at least 13 feet, bridges over local roads may have substantially less overhead clearance and may be unmarked. Be very careful when deciding to go under roadway or railroad overpasses, because many built in the 1920s are too low to accommodate today's RVs. Be willing and prepared to stop and turn around or take alternate routes.

— Share driving. This reduces the risk of driving while tired and enables RVers to arrive at their daily destination with lots of energy.

— Make a list of possible rest stops, fuel stops, and food stops along the route, designated by exit or mile markers.

— Exit and truck stop guides are invaluable for finding RV-friendly locations (e.g., locations that provide easy entrance and egress, lots of maneuvering space, separate RV pumps, RV dump stations, etc.). We recommend that you highlight the appropriate stops in your exit or truck stop guide.

— Take extra care when parking your RV in supermarket or mall parking lots. Try to park away from other vehicles and make sure that your RV is not jutting into driving lanes or blocking other vehicles. Notify the store/shopping center management if you will be there for more than a short period. RVers should request permission for overnight stays and be aware that staying overnight in parking lots is illegal in some communities.

— Use a second person and your RV's available features, including adjustable power mirrors, rear-mounted video camera and driver monitor, and sonar detection devices to help monitor tight clearances for both height and rear corners. A five-minute delay for waiting vehicles is much preferable to creating a situation where you cause hundreds or thousands of dollars of body damage to your RV or another driver's vehicle. People who wait for you to safely move your RV will appreciate your "thank you for waiting" wave.

— Because we know the dangers of using a cell phone while driving, we strongly recommend that the copilot make and receive the cellular calls while the RV is in motion. If there is no copilot, wait until you can safely stop to use the cell phone. More and more communities across the country are making the use of a cellular phone while driving a traffic infraction.

— Don't forget to shift out of overdrive on long grades, especially if you're towing. Also, visually check the tow vehicle and connections at each stop.

— Do not rush refueling activities, and pay very close attention to what is being pumped and where it is going. Unfortunately, the fill necks on some RVs could be labeled more clearly. Particular care should be exercised when refueling in bad weather, poor light, or at night.

— Check oil, water, transmission, power steering, and power brake fluid levels, and air pressure as required. It's a lot easier to add missing fluids or air at a stop than to have a breakdown or flat on the road.

— Follow a schedule that does not make you feel rushed, tired, or seems to require driving excessive distances.

— If you cannot plan a route that avoids congested areas, try to avoid all commuting hours. These are predictable in most areas, but can also differ. For instance, in Washington, D.C., and its suburbs, commuting starts at about 6:00 A.M. and continues until about 9:30 A.M. In the afternoon, you will get into commuter traffic between 3:30 P.M. and 6:00 P.M. You can either travel very early in the morning or after all commuter traffic is normally completed. On holiday weekends or heavy vacation travel periods, we've found, traveling up and down the East Coast, that we have to hit the road at about 5:30 A.M. in congested areas.

— Be cautious when making lane changes and use your mirrors, rear camera if appropriate, and signals. When the lane you want to enter is clear, put your signal on and move over; do not delay after turning on your signal. We have found that some autos will try to pass if you don't change lanes promptly when the lane is clear.

Things to Avoid While Driving an RV

All RVers have a story they're not quite sure they want to tell. However, it's important to tell other RVers in detail about embarrassing moments so that

A Lidstone Law of RVing:
RVers should not rush refueling activities and should pay very close attention to what is being pumped and where it is going. Unfortunately, the fill necks on some RVs could be labeled more clearly. Particular care should be exercised when refueling in bad weather, poor light, or at night.

Ed Cote, owner of Sarasota RV Storage and Repair, told us he has several instances every year of RVers putting fuel in water tanks, water in fuel tanks, and using the wrong fuel (gasoline or diesel) in the fuel tank. All of these situations can cause extensive, expensive, and potentially dangerous damage.

An RVer experiencing any of these di$a$ter$ must immediately stop the RV, shut everything down, and contact an RV repair facility before doing anything else.

they might not have to learn the hard way. The stories and events we relate in this chapter really happened.

Stop and Check Before You Pump or Fill

A couple in southwest Florida found out the hard way that on too-short observation, all filler necks seem to look alike. When the RVers were close to home after a trip, the husband topped off the fuel in preparation for their next trip. While closing up the RV, the husband added more water to the toilet to help make sure black water odors did not get into the RV (the toilet seal would allow the bowl to empty over several weeks of storage). He smelled a strange odor. He ran some water from several faucets, thinking it was a toilet problem, and smelled the same strong chemical odor.

He soon realized that he had not checked the gas gauge after filling the gas tank. On his Class A rig, the gas tank fill neck is next to the fill neck for the fresh water tank. Unfortunately, he had inadvertently added about 30 gallons of unleaded gas to the fresh water tank. He brought the rig over to his RV service facility in Sarasota, Florida, the first thing the following day.

By then, the gasoline had caused extensive damage to the polyethylene fresh water holding tank, the polybutylene water lines, and the various compression fittings (the solvents soften the tank and lines, causing leakage). The repairs required replacement of the complete fresh water plumbing system, except for the faucets, including the tank and all water lines and fittings. Although the cost of the parts was approximately $300, the high number of labor hours to get access to plumbing lines and replace every fitting ran the total cost of repairs to almost $1,500.

Fast Food Drive-Through = Driving's Through (for a While?)

An RVer pulled up to the speaker in the drive-through lane at a fast food outlet in Chicago. He asked the drive-through clerk if his RV could go under the overhead barriers safely. A voice responded, "Sure! No problem!" The driver continued through and promptly bumped into the overhanging guard and caused several thousand dollars of damage to his air-conditioners and rubber roof.

Communication about tight spaces is important, but you are ultimately reponible for your RV. If you have a concern or doubt about sufficient overhead clearance for your RV at fast food outlets, banks, parking lots, local road overpasses, or any other "low-bridge" or narrow space: stop and park in an open area and check it yourself. While local people will try to be helpful, only you know the height of your RV.

I "Know" the Holding Tank Is Empty

The owner of a local RV repair and storage facility services a large RV resort in Sarasota, Florida, that has many seasonal guests. As most of the rigs sit for extended times while the owners are up North, the repair service is sometimes called because of problems with holding tanks when the owners return. Gate valves that stick are generally the problem.

Before beginning work, the RV technician always first asks the RV owner, "Is the tank empty?" Too often, the RVer quickly affirms and assures the technician that the tank being serviced was emptied "just before you got here" or "half an hour ago," or the RVer says, "We just got here and the tank's been empty since last season." About half a dozen times a year, the technician proceeds to begin removing the defective gate valve and gets hit with 15–20 gallons of gray water (annoying) or black water (more than annoying) while a stunned and sheepish RVer can only say, "I really thought it was empty."

Knowing that travelers and seasonal visitors sometimes forget when the tanks were last emptied, the RV service shop's employee now brings a change of clothes and some disinfectant. He also spreads a large tarp under any RV needing gate valve work, even if the customer is "sure" the tank is empty. Do RVers really need to put repair people through this trouble? Keeping the IBM motto "THINK" in mind, the RVer can prevent a situation in which the service technician is unnecessarily hit by a deluge of dirty water.

Taking Your RV Off the Road

Sure, but don't do it. The problem isn't taking your RV off the road, it's getting it back on.

Do not take the RV onto any surface unless you are positive that other large, heavy vehicles have pulled into the area and backed out with no difficulty. There are many surfaces that appear safe and will support the weight of a car, but will bury an RV to the axles, especially if it is towing.

I missed a turnoff on a dead-end road while going to the RV park at the Cheatham Naval Annex in Williamsburg, Virginia. The turn was properly marked, but the sign was unobtrusive on account of the attractive housing area near the camping area, so it just didn't register with us. When we realized there wasn't enough space to turn the RV and toad around, I had to make a decision. I noticed that if I were to drive about 100 yards across a flat, grassy, and sandy area, I would meet a paved road that intersected with the road back, and I wouldn't have to disconnect the toad. To check the terrain, I got out and walked around. I thought the perfectly flat, sandy area was hardpan, so I advised my wife that it would be fine to drive on.

I pulled off and the RV moved through the grassy area with no problem and onto the sandy area with no problem. The front RV wheels made ruts in the sandy area that were about 2 inches deep. Unfortunately, within 5 feet, the rear wheels settled in about 10 to 12 inches deep. The sandy surface that had appeared hard and smooth because of an earlier rain was in actuality a volleyball court, filled with loose sand about 18 inches deep. The sand could support the 6,000 pounds on the front axle, but not the 11,000 pounds on the rear axle. So although I avoided the ten minutes to unhook and reconnect the toad, we lost an hour waiting for the tow truck and listening to the good-natured chuckling of the tow truck driver and the sightseers who appeared instantly out of nowhere.

Lesson learned the hard way: If your intuition tells you that something doesn't look or feel quite right, follow your intuition, because the situation is fraught with peril. If you think you might have to block traffic briefly to check out a situation or to remove the toad to get out of a situation, then block traffic or remove the toad.

Overhead Clearance

While camping in Meredith, New Hampshire, an RVer who had the same Winnebago Chieftain as ours came over to chat. At one point in the conversation he asked if our rear roof air-conditioning unit was noisy. After listening to our air-conditioner run, he said that our unit was much quieter than his and that he would be stopping back at the dealer to have it checked. We asked if his air-conditioning unit had always been noisy. He said no, not the original one installed by the factory. What happened to it, you wonder?

Well, he lived in northern Massachusetts, about two hours away from the Meredith area, and was very familiar with the local scenic New England roads. While driving on a familiar road one day, he approached a railroad overpass he'd driven through uneventfully many times before in his 1988 Winnebago. The road under the overpass made a slight S curve going under the tracks, to the right going in, and to the left coming out. As he was about halfway into the overpass with his new 1998 Winnebago, which is higher than the older model, he realized too late that he had never been through it in the new RV.

Initially, the front air-conditioning unit cleared as he went through. However, as he pulled through and bore left, the right rear shifted toward the right side of the overhead, and he heard a sickening thump-slash-bump, and then the totally unexpected sound of loud wind rushing through the Winnebago. The air-conditioning unit had sheared off cleanly, with only a few minor scratches on the fiberglass roof and some dangling wires and insulation.

Negotiating That Narrow Two-Way Road in Your Wider-Than-Most-Cars RV

Once while leaving a campground with narrow roads in southern Georgia early in the morning in dim light, we found ourselves facing a large fifth-wheel coming at us. In our memories now, the truck towing the fifth-wheel seemed to be speeding at us in a manner similar to the way the truck roared through the suburban neighborhood in the film *The World According to Garp*. At least, that's the way Barbara remembers it. The fifth-wheel was being towed by a medium-duty tow vehicle, and the determined driver seemed all hunched over the wheel and oblivious. We got nervous. Since there wasn't room for both vehicles to pass, I made the decision to pull left into an adjacent, empty pull-through site.

Watching the rear bumper area closely, I pulled slowly into the site at between 1 and 2 miles per hour. I saw the right rear bumper brush a bush, but thought the contact was no big problem, right? WRONG! The light was dim, the bush was a shrub, and we could not see the 30-inch-high sawed-off telephone pole that was obscured by vines growing all around it. The obstacle had been originally pounded into the ground to block an old exit road, which was now completely overgrown from lack of use. Under these circumstances, we had no idea the pole was there until the tip of the bumper clipped into it, causing $600 worth of damages.

Although I almost always check out all departure routes out of a campground before we actually leave, I neglected doing it this time. We now have a $600 reminder as to one of the reasons we always take a walk around the campground or resort.

Getting Through New York City in an RV

While camping in the Florida Keys, we met some RVers from Ohio who had a challenging time getting through New York City. They were traveling from Cape Cod to southern New Jersey in a 36-foot Bounder with a car in tow and had come down I-95. This was their first foray into the roads, traffic, and challenges of driving in metropolitan New York City.

Our adventurous friends had planned on going west on the Bruckner and Cross Bronx Expressways to go over the upper deck of the George Washington Bridge. Unfortunately, they missed the I-95 change from south to west. They had no choice but to continue south on I-95 over the Throgs Neck Bridge into Queens County.

Their peregrinations took them over a bridge across Long Island Sound, and, dazed and confused, they wound up on the Cross Island Parkway. Grateful to see a small parking area adjacent to the parkway, they pulled over to figure out where to go next.

While our friends were reading maps, a New York City police car pulled up. The RVers informed the "friendly" police officers that they had missed their turn and were lost. With Ohio politeness, they asked for directions to continue on their way. The police officers abruptly informed them that RVs were not allowed on the parkway and, ignoring their request for directions and information, wrote them a traffic ticket. The officers were kind enough, however, to tell our shocked midwestern friends to get off at the next exit because the RV would probably not clear the overpasses above the parkway.

Fortunately, a construction worker in the area saw their distress and came over to provide the directions they needed to work their way across Queens and Brooklyn and to continue into New Jersey over the Verrazano Bridge.

The motto in situations like this should be: "When in doubt, don't. And when maybe in doubt, don't."

CHAPTER 12

How to Keep from Getting Lost

Sunday drives in the countryside are fun, but not when you're towing a car, you've already driven 300 miles that day, and you're not quite sure where the campground is located. To make sure this never happens, use and read your maps and road atlases thoroughly before and during any trip.

Road Atlases and Maps

RVers traveling through multiple states will find a good road atlas helpful. The atlas maps are generally much larger and easier to read than campground directory maps, and flipping pages is easier than unfolding individual state maps.

Road atlases are widely available at bookstores, RV supply stores, and discount stores such as Kmart and Wal-Mart. They frequently come with discount coupons worth more than the cost of the atlas. A well-known example is the *Rand McNally Road Atlas,* which comes in several editions. An excellent atlas for RVers is the *Atlas and Travel Planner,* published by Travel Life Books.

Excellent maps of each state are generally available at no cost in the welcome stations and visitor centers on the Interstate Highway System. These are very detailed maps, frequently including campground, state park, and tourist information of great value to the RVer.

Free Trip Routing and Mapping Services

For RVers without access to computers, the major RV user groups—including Good Sam and FMCA—and manufacturer user groups will provide free trip routing. RVers who are members of AAA or other similar service providers can also obtain trip routing services from those organizations.

RVers with computers or PDAs with internet access can get on-line mapping and trip routing services from a number of websites. Mapping services simply display the map of a specific area. Trip routing services display a map of the trip (from designated start to designated finish) and an itinerary for each leg (change of roads) between the start and finish points. The trip routing itineraries are excellent, but all of the maps only fill a portion of the screen and are hard to read.

It's important to try out the different sites to see which ones you like. They are all easy to use, generally only requiring a location for mapping, and a start location and end location for trip routing. For trip routing, it takes less than fifteen to twenty seconds to get a response. All of the sites below provide a map and list the mileage and estimated time for each leg. You should print out the itinerary once you're satisfied and use it in conjunction with your road atlas, map, or full-screen computer map (see next section).

Different websites have different flavors. For example, the Good Sam site allows you to display all campgrounds and services along a route. Some sites provide both mapping and trip routing, while others provide only mapping or trip routing. We suggest you access the following sites to see which you are most comfortable with and which provide you with the information you need:

- www.delorme.com—click on "EarthaMaps" for mapping service, open to everybody.
- www.goodsamclub.com—trip routing for Good Sam members.
- www.mapquest.com—MapQuest trip routing, open to everybody, provides extensive information, access to phone directories, city guides, etc.
- www.mapblast.com—MapBlast trip routing, open to everybody, access to phone directories, downloads to PDAs, etc.
- www.koakampgrounds.com—KOA trip routing, open to everybody, uses MapQuest and allows you to display KOA Kampgrounds along the route.
- www.expedia.com—Expedia trip routing, open to everybody, travel information regarding hotels, airlines, etc.
- maps.yahoo.com—Yahoo! Maps and trip routing, open to everybody
- www.randmcnally.com—Rand McNally trip routing, open to everybody, uses MapBlast and provides access to their on-line store for all their products.

— www.roadguides.com—North American Roadguides trip planning and mapping service, open to everybody, uses MapBlast and has extensive information and links to travel-related websites.

Low-Cost Software Applications

RVers with computers and those in the process of buying one can consider low-cost options for computerized campground directories, mapping and routing, and exit information. These software applications cost approximately $20–$50 each and are invaluable for trip planning.

The *Trailer Life RV Campground Finder* CD-ROM provides detailed street maps of the entire United States. It also provides all of the campground listings and information for the United States, Canada, and Mexico included in the Trailer Life campground directory. The CD-ROM does not provide any trip routing or positioning capability and only lists limited other information. Updating is annual and the cost is about $20. Because *Trailer Life RV Campground Finder* provides no maps of Canada or Mexico, you will need to ensure you have the appropriate maps and campground directories when you visit those areas.

There are several excellent and inexpensive CD-ROM software packages of value for mapping and trip routing. DeLorme's *AAA Map'n'Go, Street Atlas USA*, and *Street Atlas USA Road Warrior Edition*, Microsoft's *Streets & Trips*, and Rand McNally's *TripMaker* software provide mapping and trip routing. These software packages also provide extensive information on attractions, recreational facilities, hotels, restaurants, business, public and educational services, and a limited number of campgrounds. *Streets & Trips* includes all 9,000 of the campgrounds listed in Woodall's campground directory. Keep in mind that DeLorme's *Street Atlas* only covers the United States.

Mapping and routing software packages can also link to the internet to download current scheduled construction activity, roadwork, and weather. In addition, they can also use a GPS receiver to provide real-time navigation and location data (see next section).

CD-ROM mapping and routing software products sell for approximately $20–$50. They are updated annually and are frequently available with rebates.

They can be obtained directly from the software developers or from many of the office supply and computer stores. Although the different offerings share the same overall functions, each has its own feel and idiosyncrasies. As with campground directories, we recommend that RVers try out more than one package; experimentation allows you to select the one you are most comfortable with. We, along with many other RVers, use more than one package because the lists of attractions, restaurants, motels, and so forth seem to vary. Because of the low cost of the products and the availability of discounts and rebates, you can purchase more than one package and still not spend much money.

RVers who own PDAs should be aware that trip routing information can be downloaded to the PDA from some trip routing websites and computer trip routing programs.

Powering Up Your GPS and Other Devices

Most RVs have at least two easily accessible 12-volt (DC) outlets in the cab area. The engine batteries and the coach batteries power the 12-volt (DC) power system in RVs. The engine batteries provide power, usually to the cigarette lighter outlet, whenever the ignition switch is turned on. The coach batteries usually provide one or more 12-volt (DC) outlets in the cab area that provide 12-volt (DC) power all the time (as long as the battery-disconnect feature is not engaged). When we first started taking long trips, we always seemed to need more outlets than the two we had for 12-volt–powered items, such as:

— Cell phone adapter/charger
— GPS device used with laptop
— Portable inverter for 120-volt (AC) power
— 12-volt (DC) cooler
— PDA charger

The solution we chose is the multiple-outlet jack available from office supply and auto parts stores. Multiple-outlet jacks plug into a single 12-volt (DC) outlet to provide two or three 12-volt (DC) outlets for a cost of $10–$15. They are generally found in the computer and portable devices sections of the office supply stores.

Low-Cost RV GPS Systems

RVers who have computers or PDAs also have low-cost options for computerized trip planning, maps, routing, and access to a global positioning satellite (GPS) system. Using GPS technology, the location of your RV is displayed on the on-screen map with a colored circle, which is a fun and useful feature to have on your computing device. Enabling satellites move in geostationary orbits around the globe and provide positional information to any GPS receiver with an accuracy of about 100 yards.

Low-cost navigation or GPS systems include the aforementioned DeLorme's *Street Atlas USA* or *AAA Map'n'Go*, Microsoft's *Streets & Trips*, and Rand McNally's *TripMaker* software. These products provide navigation support via a small GPS receiver attached to your laptop computer or PDA. The GPS receivers cost approximately $100–$120, and are available from a variety of hardware and software manufacturers, including DeLorme, Garmin, Trimble, Magellan, Rockwell, and Rand McNally. The GPS units may also be purchased at a discount when bundled with the mapping and routing computer software. In addition, the GPS units can be used with a variety of computer software mapping and routing applications.

A major advantage of the low-cost GPS systems running on a laptop is that the display is much larger than the display sizes available for the PDAs and the screens on the mid-range and high-end solutions.

The software and GPS receiver can be used anywhere your computer or PDA is located—RV, home, business, or car. (Again, if you are going to use a computer in your RV, we strongly recommend that you choose a laptop on account of its light weight, small size, and ability to handle bumps and jiggles.) Be sure to review the individual specifications of the software as compared to your computer or PDA to ensure compatibility and satisfactory results. The mapping and GPS software and GPS receivers are available from the product developers, office supply stores, and computer software stores.

The GPS receiver communicates with global positioning satellites to display your actual RV location in real time along the travel route. The device also provides voice instructions as to exits and turns along the route. If you decide to use a laptop computer with a GPS receiver, you will need a high-intensity (active matrix or TFT) display for maximum legibility.

Mid-Range Navigation Systems

This section covers the mid-range GPS solutions (which can cost from $300 up to about $1,200–$1,500) utilizing handheld or portable devices that can be used in any vehicle. More expensive options for computerized trip planning, maps, routing and access GPS systems available in turnkey devices that include both the hardware and software are covered in the next section. These high-end systems are not portable, and the equipment, displays, and antennas usually require professional installation in the RV.

In addition to the GPS device, you may need regional data cartridges or software CDs with nationwide mapping information and the availability of a laptop or personal computer. The computer, if required, is used to extract data from the software CDs and transfer it to a data cartridge for use in the handheld device.

Mid-range solutions are currently available from Garmin and Magellan. Both providers use a combination of hardware, software, cables, and accessories to provide mapping and locating services.

The central hardware device is a handheld or small GPS device (costing $300–$600) with a black-and-white or color screen that displays a map showing your location. Any device selected should be capable of being held in a mounting bracket. There are also smaller handheld devices (costing approximately $125–$300) that are fine for hiking. The GPS device has a receiver, computer processor, and memory that must perform four functions:

- Receive location information from the nearest GPS satellites
- Use preloaded mapping information stored in the GPS device

— Compare GPS data received from the satellite to the preloaded mapping information about the general area
— Generate a location map and indicate your position on the display

The GPS device contains a built-in receiver that locks onto the signal from the nearest GPS satellites. If the signal is blocked because of the physical location of the GPS device in the RV or vehicle, the GPS device will have to be connected to a remote external antenna ($80–$100 and up). The advantage of GPS devices is their small weight and size, but their very small LCD screens may be unpalatable to some.

Mapping data is downloaded into the GPS device from a data cartridge or a laptop or desktop computer. The data cartridges are available from the GPS device manufacturer for specific geographic regions of the country. You can also use a software CD with the mapping information for the entire country or region ($50–$100) and a laptop or personal computer to select the information to be downloaded. You have to use a cable connection or other device to copy the desired information to the GPS device.

When considering purchase of a mid-range GPS device for navigation and mapping needs, you should consider several possibilities. For instance, if you currently own a mid-range GPS device, you might be able to upgrade it with cartridges and other components that meet your needs. You also have to decide between a color or gray-scale display. You should try out and evaluate the brightness, size, and readability of the display in bright sunlight. Lastly, you might decide that a laptop or desktop computer is also needed, in addition to the GPS device.

If you decide upon a GPS device and possibly a remote antenna, you will also have to consider requirements and costs for accessories such as:
— Batteries
— Cigarette lighter adapter
— Cables
— Carrying case
— Mounting brackets

- Miscellaneous cables
- Nationwide mapping software and databases
- Metropolitan mapping and location databases
- Blank data cartridges

The major advantage of GPS devices is their portability, but the RVer must decide if the value obtained is worth the cost.

High-End Navigation Systems

There are several high-end specialized navigation systems (which can also provide a PDA with e-mail, mapping, GPS, CD player, stereo, and VCR components all in one package) that can be installed permanently in the RV. They cost a minimum of $1,500, but total costs can easily run anywhere from $2,500–$3,000. The overall cost depends on the vendor and which features are selected, but it is sure to cost $500–$1,000 for installation and related software.

High-end specialized navigation systems generally consist of a display unit with an LCD or active matrix screen, a system box that might include a CD drive, and a remote or external antenna. They usually require or employ multiple mapping CDs.

Current providers of high-end navigation systems include:
- Blaupunkt GPS navigation and audio system
- CARiN navigation system
- Alpine navigation and information systems
- Clarion AutoPC—includes stereo radio, CD player, PDA with e-mail, and GPS
- Datus Personal Navigator—for business and commercial use, includes wireless communications capability
- Magellan GPS Vehicle Navigation and Driver Information System
- Pioneer GPS in-dash navigation system with a variety of options (also available in a stand-alone configuration)

Most of these high-end products are multipurpose products developed for the luxury car market and often offer functions such as radio, CD and DVD player, TV, personal wireless communications, and e-mail. High-end systems can be purchased from Camping World and stores that carry high-end auto-motive electronics products, including Circuit City and Sound Design. We recommend that you check all possible vendors because the prices, installation costs, and service and warranty policies vary.

We recommend that RVers only strongly consider navigation products that are easy to use and that have a reasonably large and bright display screen and buttons that are reached easily. Those multipurpose products that were developed for the relatively confined spaces of an automobile might be too difficult or annoying to operate easily or effectively in a moving RV.

Suggestions

The most bang for your buck when trip planning is a good road atlas and any of the software programs for campgrounds, mapping, and trip routing. If you already own a laptop computer or PDA, and the screen is bright enough and legible, you will find what you need with the low-cost approach. If you want to use GPS software with a PDA, check to see which of the three developers (DeLorme, Microsoft, or Rand McNally) provides the best package and price for your needs.

Any navigation system being used in a moving RV should be operated and controlled by the passenger. We cannot stress this too highly. These devices provide a lot of functionality but require pushing small buttons or keys, watching a small screen, and concentrating on something other than safe driving.

If you're not sure you need real-time navigation capability but you own a computer or PDA and are interested in trying out the GPS system, then consider using a GPS receiver with the DeLorme or Microsoft mapping and trip routing software CDs. They provide excellent, inexpensive routing and mapping capabilities in the RV or at home. For the additional expense of approximately $120, you can obtain real-time position data along your route. You may have to purchase a remote antenna/receiver for the RV if you don't have a clear line of sight to the satellites.

If you already own a handheld or portable GPS device and the regional map and database cartridges, but not a laptop computer, the mid-range solution is an excellent choice for you. If you do own a laptop computer in addition to these things, you might still want the mid-range approach because you could use the nationwide mapping and database CDs in lieu of purchasing multiple regional or metropolitan data cartridges. Another advantage of the mid-range approach, in either of these circumstances, is that the navigation device is small, light, and easy to use. You can carry it in your pocket and easily use it outside the RV.

If you make lots of trips, but don't like fussing with computers and transferring data, and don't own a laptop computer or don't want or need to bring one on trips, you should be evaluating the high-end solutions. The advantages of the high-end solutions are ease of use and integration of multiple features. The disadvantage is their very high cost when compared with other more economical mapping, routing, and navigation methods.

CHAPTER 13

SETTING UP AND
TAKING DOWN THE RV SITE

Orderly, predictable setup and takedown of an RV site requires attention to detail, but can help avoid major problems. Hints and suggestions for setting up and taking down your site are provided here to help you manage your comings and goings with minimum fuss and no damage.

Setting up your site involves positioning the RV on the site, hooking up utilities, lowering the jacks, extending the slideouts, raising the TV antenna or satellite dish, opening the awnings, and setting out the patio items (e.g., carpet, chairs, etc.).

Positioning the RV

Positioning the RV on the site involves backing in or pulling through to line up with the water, electric, and sewer hookups, allowing adequate clearance for slideout units. In addition, if you plan on using a satellite receiver, you will need a clear line of sight from the dish antenna to the TV satellites.

We strongly recommend that one person drive the RV while a second person stands outside, in clear view of the driver, to check the site for obstructions, other campers, children, and animals as the RV is positioned. Monitor all close clearances for both height and width, including air-conditioning units and upper and lower rear corners.

Obstructions include overhanging branches, trees, rocks or boulders, utility hookups, and any items that could come into contact with the RV as you position it on the site. The second person, the adjustable feature on your mirrors, the rear-mounted video camera and driver monitor up front, sonar detection devices, two-way communicators if you have them, and your common sense can all tell you if obstructions have to be dealt with before you pull forward or back up.

If you sense that something may be wrong, stop, get out of the RV, and walk the area of concern to get a clear view. You will then be more able to get a handle on what you have to do to get a straight shot at your site.

Don't worry about blocking other RVs and don't be concerned if you're running late. Every RVer shares your concerns about tight spots and will be glad to wait or assist. Because of the mass, weight, and power of an RV, you can cause substantial damage to your rig by brushing against a tree, rock, or obstruction without feeling, hearing, or noticing anything while it's happening.

Most campgrounds and resorts mount the water hookup on a 4-by-4-inch post. During daylight hours, you may want to consider putting a large visible object such as a picnic cooler or a water bucket on top of or next to the water hookup to help the driver see it in the side-view mirror. At night, you can consider hanging a "snake" flashlight or similar light on the water hookup and any other obstructions that the driver should be alerted to.

Once you're positioned in the site, before doing anything else, set the RV parking brake, put the transmission lever in "Park" position, and put the wheel chocks in place.

Hooking Up Utilities

A full-service site might provide water, sewer, electricity, TV cable, and possibly a phone hookup. We recommend completing these hookups before lowering jacks or opening slideouts because you may find it necessary to move the RV as you go through the hookups.

Water Hookup

The suggested sequence of steps for hooking up the water supply is as follows:

- Make sure the internal RV water pump is turned off before hooking up to the campground or resort water system.
- Turn off the campground or resort water supply faucets.
- Install pressure regulator to campground water supply.
- Connect Y fixture if using two hoses.
- Connect water hoses to the pressure regulator on the water supply, or directly to the water supply if you do not use a pressure regulator.

- Connect fresh water hose to RV with quick-disconnect fitting.
- Leave black water tank flushing hose disconnected at RV (only connect this hose when actually flushing tanks).
- Turn on campground water supply.
- Close gray water holding tank valve (to provide water to flush sewer hose).
- Enter RV and run water through all fixtures to eliminate any trapped air.
- Turn on hot water heater.

We recommend that you carry the following items for your water hookups:
- Quick-disconnect fittings on all RV-mounted water hookup fixtures
- 25-foot and 50-foot lengths of $5/_8$-inch- or $1/_2$-inch-diameter fresh water hoses with quick-disconnect fittings
- Water pressure regulator (see below)
- Threaded Y plumbing fixture (see below)
- 25-foot length of black water tank flushing hose with quick-disconnect fittings
- Spare 25-foot water hose

The plumbing system in your RV is made out of plastic pipe that uses glued and/or compression fittings. It is rated to work safely at pressures up to about 50 PSI. While all RVers are annoyed about campgrounds with low water pressure, we frequently forget that other campgrounds actually design their water systems so that every site will have adequate pressure even when the campground is bursting at the seams on holiday weekends. These campgrounds may have water pressure as high as 100 PSI. That pressure can rupture hoses and internal RV plumbing lines (flooding the site and the RV interior—BIG $$$). Pressure regulators that cost $8–$16 can prevent that problem.

Another important consideration is the use of your black water tank's flushing system with its own hose, if it has one. You can use a Y fixture at the water hookup for the second hose.

The use of quick-disconnect fittings saves wear and tear on your RV plumbing fixtures because the quick-disconnect is threaded onto the RV fixture and left there. The second half is mounted to the hose and snaps onto the first part. These fittings also provide faster connect and disconnect times.

If you have a black water tank flushing system with its own supply hose, we recommend that you hook it up at the Y fitting but leave it disconnected in the utilities bay. You can snap it on (using the quick-disconnect fittings) when you flush the tanks, and then snap it off when you are finished. This will prevent leaving the flushing hose running if you forget to turn off the water supply. Also, do not ever use this hose as the fresh water supply hose. Back flushing sometimes occurs when the water supply is turned off, which could allow water run-off from the black water tank to get into this hose and contaminate it.

If you find the water pressure at the campground or resort to be low, turn off the outside water supply and switch to the RV fresh water pump to see if it generates higher pressure. If the internal RV pump provides better pressure, then:

⸺ Fill up the RV fresh water tank.
⸺ Turn off the outside water supply.
⸺ Use the internal 12-volt (DC) water pump and fresh water tank.
⸺ Refill the fresh water tank as required.

This procedure is also recommended if you do not have a pressure regulator and find yourself in a campground or resort with high water pressure.

Using the RV fresh water tank for water supply in the above situations has the advantage of providing safe water pressure and flushing out the fresh water tank and lines.

Sewer Hookups

RVs have a gray water holding tank to hold the sink and bathtub/shower waste (gray) water and a black water tank to hold toilet waste. Each tank has a separate gate valve that empties into a common fitting with a "twist-on" dust cap. The sewer hose is attached by removing the dust cap and attaching the sewer hose in its place.

The suggested sequence of steps for hooking up the sewer hose is as follows:

— Make sure the black water holding tank gate valve and gray water holding tank gate valve are closed.
— Determine what length of hose is required.
— Get out hose and hose support (see note below).
— Connect RV end of hose.
— Connect campground end of hose to sewer hose collar or threaded coupling and connect to sewer opening.
— Put hose support under hose.

Note: A variety of hose supports to support the sewer hose between the connection at the RV and the campground sewer system are available from RV supply stores. We recommend a support that can be extended to at least 8 feet in length and preferably up to 20 feet. These supports keep the hose off the ground, aid in draining fluids out of the sewer hose, and keep the outside of the hose clean.

RVers on the road for extended trips should consider carrying the following sewer items to hook up at a site:

— 10-foot length of 3-inch-diameter sewer hose with connectors to drain black and gray water holding tanks
— Additional 20-foot lengths of 3-inch-diameter sewer hose
— Additional sewer connector fittings to enable connecting multiple 10-foot and 20-foot sections
— Disposable vinyl or latex gloves for attaching, removing, and cleaning hoses
— Sewer hose rubber collar or threaded collar adapter
— Sewer hose support (between RV and sewer fitting)
— Holding tank deodorants and chemicals
— Spray bottle of bathroom/kitchen cleaner and paper towels or old dish towels for tidying up the utility and hookup area

Electric Hookup

The suggested sequence of steps for hooking up electric power is as follows:

— Make sure the RV generator is turned off.

— Turn off the campground circuit breaker.

— Hook up the RV end of the power cord.

— Hook up the campground (power supply) end of the power cord.

— Turn on the campground circuit breaker.

— Check the polarity and voltage of the 120-volt (AC) power (see note below).

RVers on the road for extended trips should consider carrying the following items:

— 25 feet of 30 amp or 50 amp electric hookup cables for 120-volt (AC) power

— Voltage meter and/or polarity tester for 120-volt (AC) system

— 25-foot power extension cord to plug into the existing 25-foot power cord (for a total of 50 feet)

— 50 amp–30 amp adapter (in the event the campground does not have 50 amp power)

— 30 amp–20 amp adapter (in the event the campground does not even have 30 amp power)

— Portable 140 watt–300 watt inverter for TV or laptop computer

Note: Voltage meters ($15–$40) will indicate if the AC power supply (shore power or generator) is providing a low-voltage environment (less than 108 volts) that can damage air-conditioning units, microwave ovens, and some electric appliances. Do not use the 120-volt (AC) shore power provided by the campground or resort if a low-voltage environment exists. Notify the campground management of the condition and defer using your 120-volt (AC) appliances and equipment or use your generator until the problem is resolved. Polarity testers (approximately $10) will indicate if the shore power has reversed polarity, thereby creating an unsafe electrical condition. Voltage and polarity should be checked when RV is initially hooked to shore power, and voltage should be checked periodically while you are in a campground and whenever a potential of low voltage is suspected or actually occurs (e.g., if you experience dimming lights, etc.).

Cable TV and Telephone

Many campgrounds and resorts have cable TV available, and a limited number are starting to provide very convenient telephone access directly to each RV site. The suggested steps for hooking up cable TV and telephone are as follows:

- Set the internal video control center to "Cable-TV."
- Turn the TV antenna signal amplifier switch to the off position.
- Connect the external coax cable to the RV and to the campground cable TV adapter.
- Connect the external phone line to the RV and to the campground connector.
- Connect the internal phone line to the internal RV phone jack and handset.

We suggest you carry the following items to make use of these facilities:

- Installed coax adapter in RV utility bay or other convenient location
- 50 feet of TV coax cable (RV to campground connector)
- 5-foot coax TV cable for wall-mounted bedroom TV
- Installed external telephone jack adapter in RV utility bay or other convenient location connected to telephone jack inside RV
- 50 feet of telephone line with adapters on each end
- Telephone line and telephone handset for use in the RV

Jacks/Air Bag Stabilizers and Slideouts

Many of the RVs in use today have leveling and stabilization systems that allow the RVer to level the RV and lift the weight of the RV off its suspension system after positioning it on the campsite. This stops the RV from "jiggling" as you walk around and may also be required for proper operation of the RV refrigerator. Two systems in use are the hydraulic systems using jacks and the air bag systems. The type of system used is generally based on the size and weight of the RV.

In addition to the stabilization systems, most of the RVs are available with one or more slideout units that extend 16 to 36 inches past the side of the RV to provide additional space in the living, kitchen and eating, and bedroom and bath areas. These may be powered hydraulically or electrically.

Be sure to follow your coach manufacturer instructions for lowering the jacks or actuating the air bag stabilization system. If you are using jacks, you may want to place blocks of wood under the jack feet if the site is not level to provide additional height and keep the jack pads from touching or sinking into the ground. If your system does not have automatic leveling, you should use the levels available in camping supply stores to make sure the RV is level side-to-side and front-to-back.

When leveling the coach, it is important that you do not "twist" the chassis. Twisting the chassis can adversely affect your slideout unit, loosen things up, pop windshields out of place, and possibly cause leaks as panels flex. This can occur on sites that are not level. Your coach documents will cover this problem in detail.

The suggested steps for operating jacks and air bag stabilizers to level the coach are as follows:

- Make sure the RV parking brake is set, transmission lever is in "Park" position, and wheel chocks are in place.
- Turn ignition switch to the mode recommended by the coach manufacturer.
- Ensure that area under jacks is unobstructed, reasonably level, and firm.
- Put blocks under jack feet as required.
- Extend jacks or actuate air bag stabilizers as specified in the coach manual instructions.
- Hang flag or other indicator on steering wheel or gearshift to indicate that leveling system has been actuated.
- Turn ignition switch to the off position if power is not required to extend a slideout.

After completing the leveling activities, you are ready to extend the slideouts. Check the area around the RV to make sure there are no obstructions, including low-hanging tree branches that can get tangled in or damage the slideout awning.

The suggested steps for extending slideouts are as follows:

- Release any internal slideout locking travel latches specified in the coach manual instructions.
- Turn ignition switch to appropriate mode.
- Ensure area is clear, including above the slideout.
- Extend slideouts as indicated in coach instructions.
- Hang flag or other indicator on steering wheel or gearshift to indicate that slideout is extended.
- Turn ignition switch to off position.

Stove and Hot Water Heater

Now you are ready to turn on the external valve of the exterior propane tank to provide gas for the range, oven, and hot water. Because air may have accumulated in the gas line, it takes fifteen or twenty seconds to provide adequate gas flow for these appliances.

You should open a window and the overhead vent and turn on the stove exhaust fan prior to turning on a burner to clear the line for the range and oven. This will help get rid of unburned propane gas that comes out before the burner lights. Gas hot water heaters are already vented to the outside and no action is required regarding ventilation while waiting for the burner assembly to ignite.

Satellite TV

If your coach has an automatic-sensing satellite dish, it can be activated as soon as the TV, satellite dish, and receiver have power. RVers with manual satellite dishes should not set up the dish until after leveling the coach and extending the slideouts.

The various types of satellite antennas and services are discussed in the "Entertainment Media" section of Chapter 3 (Making the Trip Comfortable).

The suggested sequence of steps for enabling the satellite dish is as follows:

- Release antenna lock on satellite dish (if required).
- Set video control box to appropriate setting.
- Turn satellite receiver on.
- Set up satellite dish per manufacturer instructions.
- Hang flag or other indicator on steering wheel, gearshift, or antenna handle to indicate that satellite dish is raised (unless antenna sits under a covered dome).

TV Antenna

If you will be using your TV antenna, now is the time to set it up. The suggested steps for raising your TV antenna are as follows:
- Set the internal video control center to "Antenna."
- Turn the TV antenna signal amplifier switch to the on position.
- Turn the TV on and turn down the sound.
- Release the antenna lock, and raise and rotate the antenna to get the best picture.
- Hang flag or other indicator on steering wheel, gearshift, or antenna handle to indicate that TV antenna is raised.

The Awnings

All that's left to do is roll down the awnings, lay out the patio carpet, tables, and chairs, and start relaxing. Check for clearance and obstructions before lowering any awning.

We suggest you lower one end of the awning to facilitate water run-off and reduce the chance of awning collapse due to water collection during a thunderstorm or downpour (unless you have an awning automatic sensing system). We also recommend that you raise your awnings or use appropriate tie-downs and anchors if high winds are possible or you will be away from the RV site for more than a few minutes.

When It's Time to Head Out

Taking down the site and getting back on the road means going through the setup list of activities in reverse. We've already discussed the various factors involved in hooking up and turning on everything, so this section is primarily a checklist of activities.

While inside, do the following:

— Turn off the TV, satellite receiver, VCR, and antenna amplifier switch.
— Lower TV antenna or satellite dish antenna (if raised).
— Remove flags or other indicators on steering wheel, gearshift, or antenna handle that indicated antennas were raised.
— Turn off oven burners and stove.
— Turn off hot water heater.
— Turn off all 120-volt (AC) appliances.
— Remove all loose items on counters, end tables, bed stands, bathroom, etc., and store in appropriate places.
— Make sure all doors and cabinets are closed.
— Check levels of fresh water, gray water, and black water tanks from interior tank level indicators.

Now outside, do the following:

— Check for obstructions and low-hanging tree limbs, raise awnings, and secure awning arm locks.
— Close valve on exterior propane tank.
— Make sure patio carpet, chairs, and all loose items have been stored in bays.
— Turn off shore power circuit breaker and disconnect and store the 120-volt (AC) power cable.
— Drain black water holding tank per coach manual instructions (if required).
— Flush black water holding tank (if you have a tank flushing system).
— Close black water holding tank gate valve.
— Drain gray water holding tank (if required).
— Close gray water holding tank gate valve.
— Add water to, or drain sufficient water from, the fresh water tank to ensure enough water for traveling and use until you will next be able to hook up to a fresh water supply.

- Disconnect, rinse, and store sewer hose (use plastic garbage bag or covered container).
- Remove and store sewer hose adapter or collar.
- Fold up and store sewer hose support.
- Attach and lock outside dust cover/seal to drain.
- Disconnect and store all water hoses, pressure regulators, and any associated plumbing fixtures.
- Disconnect and store cable-TV coax and phone lines.
- Remove and store wheel chocks.
- Check to see that extended jacks are free of debris and ready to be raised.
- Check to see there are no tree limbs or other obstructions that could become tangled in the slideout unit.

Again inside, do the following:
- Pour holding tank chemicals and flush several gallons of water into the toilet for the black water holding tank.
- Check and clear any interior obstructions that could interfere with retracting the slideout.
- Turn ignition switch to appropriate mode.
- Use side-view mirrors to check that the outside area remains clear and slowly retract slideouts as indicated in coach instructions.
- Retract jacks or disengage air bag stabilizers as indicated in coach instructions.
- Set locks for slideout as indicated in coach instructions.
- Remove flags or other indicators on steering wheel or gearshift that indicated actuation of leveling system or slideout.

Again outside, do the following:
- Look beneath the coach to verify that all jacks were retracted properly and chocks were removed.
- Remove and stow any blocks that were placed under the jack feet.
- Check slideout unit closely to make sure that it has closed evenly with no debris or tree branches caught in it.

- Check that all water hoses, sewer hoses, power cords, TV coax, and phone cables have been removed.
- Climb ladder or stand far from the unit to verify that all antennas are in proper position.
- Attach toad per manufacturer instructions, check RV hitch, all connections, safety chains, and that the emergency brake, toad braking, and toad gearshift are in the proper settings (see note below).
- Check that all bay doors are properly closed and locked.
- Walk completely around the coach and look for anything you might have missed.

Note: Check your tow bar and mounting brackets closely for cracks or defects every time you attach your toad. We strongly recommend that only one person perform all toad hookup activity to ensure that no tasks are lost in the shuffle due to miscommunication.

Now go inside, wash your face and hands, get that cup of coffee, and hit the road!

– – – – – –

CHAPTER 14

RETURNING HOME

Returning home will be even more enjoyable if you have a good plan for unloading and stowing the RV according to your own unhurried schedule. Completing the following tasks will reduce the preparation time needed for the next RV trip.

On the Road

— Drain the black and gray water holding tanks, rinse them if you have the equipment in your RV, and add chemicals and several gallons of water at the last campground on the trip home. A number of truck stops, such as Flying J, have RV dump facilities. The interstate exit, truck stop, and rest area guides list locations with RV dump facilities.

— Fill the propane tank before you return home. (Flying J truck stops have separate RV pump islands for both fuel and propane.)

Note: If the temperature is below freezing, also pour a little RV anti-freeze into the holding tanks through the toilet and sink.

Back at the House

— Make sure that the valve on the exterior propane tank is turned off.

— Unload the clothes, food, personal items, and necessary support items.

— Empty and clean the refrigerator and freezer and leave the doors open until the insides are back to room temperature. Most RV refrigerators have plastic interiors, and it is difficult to remove food odors after-the-fact.

— Have any necessary RV service completed (e.g., lube and oil, repairs, etc.).

— Perform any other required preventive maintenance—see Chapter 17 (Preventive Maintenance).

— Clean the interior and exterior of the RV.

- Drain the fresh water holding tank (the chlorine breaks down over time).
- Check, clean, and reorganize the contents of all interior cabinets and all exterior storage bays.

Securing the RV Until the Next Trip

- Add the appropriate fuel stabilizer if the RV will be out of use for more than forty-five to sixty days. Fuel stabilizers prevent mold from forming in the diesel fuel as well as prevent the gasoline from deteriorating.
- Actuate the coach battery-disconnect feature (if you have one) when the RV will be unused for more than a few days.
- Add chemicals and fresh water to black and gray water holding tanks if they were drained but not treated.
- Make sure that there are several inches of water in the toilet bowl to prevent black water holding tank odors from entering the coach.
- Open the roof vents slightly to allow fresh air into the RV and to prevent mildew.
- Put on RV cover to protect finish and wheel covers to protect tires.
- Winterize the RV if required—see Chapter 18 (Storing the RV over the Winter).

The RV is now ready for the next trip.

RV Support and Services

CHAPTER 15

INSURANCE, ROAD SERVICE, WARRANTY COVERAGE, AND MEDICAL EVACUATION

Selecting and buying an RV is just the first step in taking up RVing. Another important step is to look at the various types of insurance and warranty coverage that are specialized to the needs of RVers. Because the RV is much more than just a vehicle, we found we had to consider a number of protection options, including:

— RV liability, property, collision, and uninsured motorists coverage

— Road service and towing service

— Warranty services included with the RV

— Extended warranty services

— Medical evacuation and assistance services

RV Insurance

Your RV requires liability insurance like all other motor vehicles. Obviously, you need to seriously consider the level and amount of liability, uninsured motorist, property, and collision insurance you need to cover your RV. Coverage is available from most automobile insurers, although there are also specialized carriers who primarily insure RVs including motorhomes, fifth-wheels, recreational trailers, and tow vehicles.

The specialized insurers are more familiar with the unique RV insurance needs than most of the insurers who primarily insure cars and personal vehicles. All of the major RV user groups provide access to the specialized insurers. You can also find them advertised in the various RV publications such as the Good Sam *Highways* magazine and the Camping World catalogs.

Considerations to help you decide whether to use your automobile insurer or a specialized carrier include:

— What is the premium?

— Will they insure you as a full-time RVer and, if so, what does that include? (see note 1 on page 167)

- What coverage is provided for personal items in the RV in case of total loss?
- What type of road service is available and at what cost?
- Do they provide full replacement in case of total loss within the first five years? (see note 2 below)
- Do they pay off the full loan balance in case of total loss if it exceeds the book value? (see note 3 below)

Note 1: RVers who own homes with a homeowner's policy normally have comprehensive coverage, which includes personal liability coverage. Full-timers who do not own any residence with a homeowner's insurance policy that includes personal liability coverage should strongly review their need for this liability coverage as part of the RV insurance coverage.

Note 2: There are a select number of vehicle insurers who will guarantee a payoff sufficient to obtain a new RV in the event of a total loss, but only if the insured RV was purchased new and is less than five years old at the time of loss. This coverage must be arranged at the time the vehicle is initially insured.

Note 3: In the event of a total loss, there are a select number of vehicle insurers and institutions making RV loans who will guarantee a payoff of the outstanding RV loan balance over the life of the loan. This coverage must be negotiated at the time the vehicle is initially insured and the loan is established.

Consider notes 2 and 3 above very closely. This additional protection can normally only be obtained the first time the RV insurance is set up and the RV loan is established.

Road Service and Towing Service

We strongly recommend road and towing service to all RV owners. These services typically provide service in cases of flat tires, lockouts, minor mechanical repairs, or needing to be towed to repair facilities. We have had this coverage for our RV for the past three years and have made two service calls, one for towing the toad and the second for towing the RV. Without coverage, either of the calls would have far exceeded the three years of premiums. This type of insurance is available from RV user groups, total service support groups such as Camping World and AAA, and many of the insurance companies that provide RV liability, collision, and comprehensive coverage.

Regarding tire service for motorhomes, we cannot emphasize too strongly the need to use professionals. The fact that our Winnebago came from the factory with a spare tire but no jack left us to conclude that the manufacturer does not want us to change tires (which is fine with us). Motorhome tires are much heavier than automobile tires and they are inflated to very high pressures. The lug nuts on the RV wheels must be tightened to the correct amount of torque specified by the chassis manufacturer to ensure safe operation.

Road and towing services have the trained personnel and the necessary equipment and shop facilities to mount tires correctly. If you do change your own tires, it is imperative that you follow the chassis manufacturer instructions exactly as written and have the replaced tire rechecked at a qualified tire shop.

The annual fee for road and towing service is generally $60–$100 from the major RV services. AAA offers an excellent emergency road service to their members for an annual fee of $20 in addition to their other membership fees. You might also be able to obtain road and towing service coverage from your vehicle liability, comprehensive, and collision insurer for a very nominal rate (as low as $8–$15 per year). If you obtain coverage from your vehicle liability insurer, you should confirm that the towing agent of the insurer can provide the required towing and capability.

The level of coverage, including mileage and dollar limits, varies among providers. We urge you to read all the details thoroughly, especially any limits on distance your RV can be towed without incurring additional charges and any temporary meals, lodging, or alternative transportation coverage included in the annual fee, to determine which plan is most appropriate for your needs.

If you have to call for towing service, it is very important that you inform the provider of the length, total gross weight, and weight on front and rear axles of your RV to ensure they send out the proper towing vehicle and equipment.

Warranty Services Included with the RV

Our new RV, like all new RVs, came with a warranty, which is actually a series of warranties. The chassis manufacturer warranties the power train and chassis. The power train includes the engine, transmission, drive line, and related components. Chassis coverage includes the steering, suspension, electrical, and braking systems, and other related equipment.

The RV manufacturer warranties the coach, including front and rear caps, sidewalls, roof, and all structural components. They install a wide variety of additional systems and components, such as such as air-conditioning, furnace, hot water heater, TV, microwave, generator, and so forth, in completing the coach.

The coach warranty is normally for a specified time and mileage period (e.g., one year and 15,000 miles) for most problems, with selected coverage (roof or sidewall delamination) for a longer period. The warranties for the various individual systems and components are provided by the individual manufacturers and generally have different time periods and mileage limits than the coach warranty.

A Lidstone Law of RVing: It is very important that you not authorize any work until you have verified the warranty coverage and status of your claim. Most warranty work requires prior approval from the manufacturer before any work starts, and the work can only be performed at specified manufacturer warranty locations.

The authorized RV dealer provides most warranty service for coach problems. Serious problems will be referred directly to the coach manufacturer (necessitating a trip back to the factory). Warranty service for the various individual systems and components is available from the RV dealer, or any of the warranty providers designated by the various individual RV system component manufacturers.

As Good Sam members and avid readers of its magazine, we've noticed that *Highways* magazine regularly publishes letters from members who have experienced problems with service or repairs that were started without the specific manufacturer's approval. Although these members thought the work was or should have been covered by the manufacturer warranty, it was not. Therefore, we advise all RVers to

keep dated documentation of proof of purchase and appropriate maintenance records to address warranty problems. And remember to *always*
contact the manufacturer before work is started.

Most of the time, the RV dealer will address warranty problems or concerns related to the coach and its individual systems if the coach is still under
warranty. If the coach is out of warranty, but the failed item is still under
original warranty, you will probably be referred to an authorized warranty
provider if the dealer is not one. Warranty problems and concerns with the
chassis, power train, and related components have to be addressed by the
chassis provider.

Extended Warranty Services

Separately priced extended warranties, also known as continued service
plans, are available for new and used RVs. In addition to equipment coverage, some plans may also reimburse RV owners for limited travel-delay
expenses associated with covered equipment failure.

Coverage on new RVs is available for periods up to a total of seven years
(depending on the carrier) from the date of purchase or 80,000 miles,
whichever comes first. The coverage is slightly broader for new RVs. Used RV
coverage is available for units less than ten years old and with less than
80,000 miles at the time of application. Carriers reserve the right to require
an inspection prior to issuing coverage on a used RV that is not covered by
an extended warranty at the time of application.

The policies on used RVs are issued for periods of one to three years,
depending on the carrier. They can be renewed as long as the RV is less than
thirteen years old and has less than the maximum policy mileage limit (up to
115,000 miles for some carriers).

If you are purchasing a new RV, you might consider purchasing an
extended warranty for the maximum period of coverage, and then purchasing a second warranty that can be renewed as long as the RV is less than
thirteen years old. It's possible to have thirteen years of warranty coverage
if you stay within the mileage limits.

We purchased our first extended warranty when we bought a used motorhome because we felt the $1,800 premium for a three-year policy was an excellent value that provided peace of mind and eased any worries about major engine or transmission repairs or needing to replace air-conditioning units, furnace, or hot water heater. When we bought a new RV, we found the coverage to be even more extensive by covering a seven-year period and increasing the cost of our motorhome by about 2 percent.

Extended coverage piggybacks warranties issued with the RV upon original sale. Failed items will be repaired or replaced under the original warranty if it has not expired and on the extended warranty if the original warranty has expired. It is important to make sure that any extended warranty coverage you purchase will pay the repair facility directly (as opposed to you paying and then being reimbursed) and that your only out-of-pocket expenses will be for the deductible and any repairs not covered by the extended warranty.

Extended warranties specify components of the coach, power train, and chassis that will be covered. Coach coverage might include the water heater, waste system, fresh water system, air-conditioning, LP gas system, furnace, refrigerator, and generator. Additional coverage may be available for slide-outs, hydraulic jacks and leveling systems, and electric steps. Power train and chassis coverage may include the engine, transmission, drive axle, suspension, steering, air-conditioning, braking, electrical, electronic, heating/cooling, fuel delivery assemblies, and the chassis frame. *It is important that you read the covered items very carefully.*

Extended warranty policies are available for motorhomes, fifth-wheel trailers, recreational trailers, and tow vehicles. Many carriers will also provide excellent coverage for your tow vehicle, so owners of fifth-wheel and recreational trailers should check with the carrier. They come with a variety of deductibles and may be transferable for a nominal fee if the RV or tow vehicle is sold.

Important considerations regarding an extended warranty policy include:

- Cost—Extended warranty coverage is not cheap. It may well exceed $2,000 because RVs do break down and the warranty does cover repair, replacement, and installation services. The need for this type of coverage is based upon the condition of your RV, the mileage and time you'll be on the road, and whether you're willing to pay these expenses out-of-pocket. Bear in mind, however, that a new refrigerator can cost over $1,000, a hot water heater $500, a roof air-conditioner $700, and so on.
- Level of coverage and deductibles—Coverage is not 100 percent. You should read the policy very carefully to understand exactly what systems or parts of systems are covered by the warranty. If it's not listed, it's not covered.
- Adherence to warranty plan—Either you or someone at your repair facility must contact the warranty plan provider for instructions or guidance prior to starting any repair work or filing claims. Failure to follow warranty claim instructions may result in claims being rejected or payment being delayed by the warranty provider, leaving the RVer responsible for paying the total repair bill.

We advise that you make an extra copy of the extended warranty plan to keep in your RV. The repair facility may need it to process a claim. The more you use your RV, the more valuable will be the peace of mind provided by a good RV extended warranty policy.

Medical Evacuation and Assistance Services

Because RVing attracts many people who are retired or nearing retirement, health concerns can be primary. If you wonder whether health problems will prevent you from using and enjoying an RV, you should know that medical evacuation and assistance policies are available. This coverage might be just what you need to feel a little more at ease about traveling with possible serious or chronic health problems.

Types of services that might be provided by or available from this coverage are:

- Temporary lodging and meals for the family while evacuation arrangements are being made

- Transportation of the ill person and RV passengers or escorts by commercial flight
- Transportation of the ill person and RV passengers or escorts by appropriate dedicated aircraft or land transport
- Provision that RV will be returned to home location
- Transportation assistance to return to the RV for pickup if it has not already been returned to home location
- Transportation assistance or reimbursement for a relative or friend from home to travel to the area where the RVer is hospitalized

These policies are available from a number of commercial carriers and RV user groups. The needs of RVers are different from the average traveler because of the need to return the RV to the home location. You are encouraged to review multiple carriers to determine which most meets your individual needs.

CHAPTER 16

MANUALS AND
OTHER RV DOCUMENTS

Technical user manuals, documents, and instructions are provided by your RV manufacturer to help you operate and make use of your RV correctly and safely. They also spell out in detail the maintenance and installation requirements of the RV, as well as the major systems and components. We provide recommendations in this chapter for organizing documents and for obtaining replacement documents and supplemental information.

Some RVers find technical documents to be dry and dull, while others really enjoy digging in and getting at all the nitty-gritty mechanical specifications outlined in the brochures and manuals. Regardless of your relationship with them, these documents are your most important source of information for keeping all systems up and running in your RV. Using your documents to their fullest will keep your RV in tip-top shape while other RVs are in the shop or sitting on the shoulder of the road.

Although all motorhomes look similar, they tend to have unique design implementations that are clearly described in the coach manual. The time to find out where the circuit breaker panel or sewer hookups are located is before you put the key in the ignition.

A typical document package consists of a set of several dozen or more various manuals, booklets, and brochures provided by the:

- RV manufacturer
- Chassis and power train manufacturer
- Suppliers or manufacturers of the various mechanical, electrical, and electronic systems and accessories included with the motorhome

Your RV documents are very important. They tell you how to use, enjoy, and maintain your motorhome.

RV Manufacturer Documents

All RV manufacturers provide an operations and user manual for their products. Generally known as the coach manual, it is always the first place to look when trying to familiarize yourself with the proper operation of your RV or resolve problems using your RV. If you do not have a coach manual for your RV, contact your dealer or coach manufacturer to obtain a replacement.

You will (or should) also receive extensive information about the RV systems, accessories, and features from the individual manufacturers. The coach manual reflects not only this information, but also the accumulated experience of the RV manufacturer in evaluating various products in individual RV models. The coach manual can also provide comments and recommendations obtained from the manufacturer's RV customer base.

The coach manufacturers put substantial time and effort into writing and organizing their manuals because they know that RVers need the documents to gain a comprehensive understanding of specific RV makes and models.

The coach manual ensures that you can use your RV properly and confidently and can also reduce the number of SOS calls to the dealer and factory asking for help or registering complaints.

The coach manuals evolve over time, but are well written and well organized, easy to read, and chock full of very helpful information. Types of information covered include:

— An overview of the RV from bumper to bumper
— A review of all safety systems
— Driving techniques and safety considerations
— Proper operation and use of all dashboard, driver, and passenger compartment features and functions, and all engine and chassis systems
— Proper operation and use of all RV systems and appliances: entertainment systems, the complete plumbing and sanitation system, heating and air-conditioning system, all appliances, hookups, 12-volt (DC) and 120-volt (AC) systems, and generator
— Loading of the RV and proper use of hookup facilities

- Care and maintenance of the RV
- Storage of the RV

Chassis and Power Train Documents

The chassis and power train manufacturers (e.g., Workhorse, Ford, Freight-liner, etc.) provide service guides/owner's manuals. These documents are generally limited to the chassis, power plant and driveline, brake system, transmission, fuel system, steering and suspension systems, and battery and electrical system.

The motorhome chassis and power train service guides/owner's manuals provide extensive parts-related information, pictures, diagrams, and charts covering:

- service and maintenance schedules and tasks
- jacking and towing
- wheel and tire care
- driving tips
- troubleshooting
- repair procedures

You should review your chassis and power train service guide/owner's manual closely. This will ensure that you are aware of critical items affecting the safety, maintenance, and warranty conditions stipulated by the RV manufacturer. When aware of such things as maintenance schedules and tasks, jacking and towing procedures, wheel and tire care, and safe driving techniques, you have a leg up when discussing problems and needs with service providers.

The chassis and power train documents are more technical than the coach manual. The topics of troubleshooting and repair procedures are for people with considerable experience, expertise, and the proper tools. However, they are helpful in enabling you to more fully appreciate the complexity of the technology needed to power your RV.

As with the coach operations and use manual, contact your dealer or chassis and power train manufacturer to obtain a replacement if you don't have this important document.

Systems and Accessories Documents

The set of documents that is the thickest and possibly most intimidating on first glance is the new RV's accompanying "mountain" of booklets, brochures, charts and diagrams, and manuals covering all the RV systems, features, and appliances. Documents can be from one to a hundred pages in length each, depending on the feature or system. They can be formatted either as post-card-size booklets or full-size brochures and booklets. The documents always provide manufacturer information (sometimes sketchily) and discuss operations and use, service and maintenance, and installation requirements.

Be sure to retain these documents, because they provide specific information about all the systems and components installed in your particular RV. Information included may range from detailed wiring diagrams and troubleshooting instructions to, for instance, a one-line comment reminding you to remove a pin (almost invisible) before removing the cover on the carbon monoxide (CO) detector.

The documents for the major systems—such as the generator, leveling system, slideouts, hot water heater, oven and range, refrigerator, air-conditioning, furnace, TV, VCR, satellite and TV antennas, and toilet—will be large and detailed. Replacement documents for the major systems are generally available from the manufacturers.

However, you will also get a bunch of short documents and drawings on the safety detectors (i.e., propane, carbon monoxide, and smoke), water filtration system, thermostat, media distributor (for TV, VCR, satellite, and cable), and so forth. These documents, although rarely needed, are difficult to replace.

Generic Repair and Maintenance Manuals

Generic RV repair and maintenance publications cover the major RV systems and accessories. They also address coach and chassis and power train maintenance in general, as well as fifth-wheel and recreational trailer braking systems and towing needs.

A good RV repair and maintenance manual is a must for RV owners, especially those who do not have the original manufacturer documentation. We, along with many other RV owners, use a good repair and maintenance manual in conjunction with the technical information and documents that came with our RV.

The *RV Repair and Maintenance Manual,* by Bob Livingston, is an excellent source of information for new and experienced RVers. It carefully explains preventive and scheduled RV maintenance needs, troubleshooting and repair instructions, and toad towing considerations and requirements. The *Woodall's RV Owners Handbook* published by Woodall is another popular book for RV maintenance and tips.

Obtaining Replacement Documents

Sellers of used RVs might not be able to provide you with original RV documents, because they might have been damaged, lost, or discarded. However, if you provide the model and year of your RV, you can probably obtain replacement documents from one of the following sources:

— Authorized dealer

— Coach manufacturer

— Chassis and power train manufacturer

Organizing the Technical Documents

RV documentation can be organized into one or more three-ring binders. If a document is already bound but not punched with holes, consider punching holes in it so it can be put into a binder. We recommended the following sequence, which we have found to be useful:

— Copy of purchase contract (and extended warranty)

— Consolidated coach and chassis preventive maintenance checklists (see Appendices B and C)

— Coach manual

— Chassis and power train manual

— RV systems and accessories technical information

— Maintenance and service receipts

We also use plastic sleeves (available in office supply stores) because they are very helpful in organizing oddly sized documents, records, and receipts.

You should always keep the information binders in your RV while on the road. Having them handy while on a trip ensures that you can readily consult the documents when you need to follow up on the specifics of a system or a piece of equipment. In the case of that rare breakdown, organized documents help with troubleshooting, diagnostics, and repair. Many system documents include detailed wiring schematics, troubleshooting tips, and other installation and service information that will aid you and your repair personnel in locating and fixing a problem quickly so you can continue on your way.

- - - - -

CHAPTER 17

PREVENTIVE MAINTENANCE

Proper maintenance of your RV requires different levels of maintenance. This chapter addresses your preventive maintenance needs as well as the more complex needs addressed by scheduled and major maintenance requirement. We put this chapter together using the operations, user, and maintenance manuals, brochures, and documents that came with our Winnebago Chieftain, and we also incorporated comments and observations made by RV service shop technicians and other RVers.

What Is Preventive Maintenance?

Preventive maintenance is a series of individual inspections and the minor servicing of RV systems and components to ensure safe and effective operation, identify any needs for additional repairs or service, help ensure maximum service life, and reduce the incidence of parts and equipment failure.

To aid in the completion of your preventive maintenance activities, we provide separate checklists for the suggested chassis and power train preventive maintenance tasks and the coach-related preventive maintenance tasks. Mark up and modify these lists as appropriate for your RV's make and model. The specific actions associated with these maintenance tasks are covered in your manufacturer manuals and documents.

This section does not include any preventive maintenance for the propane-powered portions of the refrigerator, furnace, or hot water heater. We recommend that those safety-critical items be inspected and serviced at the manufacturer-recommended times by factory-authorized service facilities.

Who Does Preventive Maintenance?

Preventive maintenance actions can be completed by the RVer, RV dealer or service shop, or an appropriate chassis and power train service shop. Many of the tasks do not require special tools or complex procedures and can be completed by the RVer.

Do not assume that the RV shop will perform all necessary tasks unless they are specifically spelled out on the work order. Although the time required for each task is generally only a few minutes, the total time for a thorough preventive maintenance inspection and service can take several hours.

Service facilities will most likely charge by the hour to properly complete all the preventive maintenance checks, much as any other competent professional does. If you are using service shops for some of the preventive maintenance work, it is advantageous to use an RV dealer or service shop for the coach-related systems and accessories and to use a chassis and power train service shop for needs such as the chassis, engine, transmission, suspension, and braking and steering systems. For instance, the service personnel who do our lube and oil work at the Ford heavy-truck facility know every fitting on our chassis that was installed by Ford. They check fluid levels and look for loose fittings, hoses, and belts installed by the chassis manufacturer. However, the Ford mechanics do not necessarily know where the coach manufacturer installed the hydraulic fluid reservoir for the coach jacks and slideouts, routed the hydraulic fluid supply lines, or installed additional coach wiring harnesses, and we have that work done by the RV dealer.

RVers completing their own preventive maintenance procedures gain an improved understanding as to what makes the RV tick, and peace of mind that the RV is ready to roll.

What's the Difference Between Preventive and Scheduled Maintenance?

Scheduled and major maintenance checks are covered in the "Scheduled and Major Maintenance Needs" section of this chapter. These activities keep you in compliance with your RV's warranty conditions.

We strongly recommend that you use authorized dealers that have good reputations within the community and come recommended by other RVers, because scheduled and major maintenance checks are complicated and require elaborate procedures, special tools, and safety precautions. Authorized dealers have the knowledge and trained service personnel, as well as factory support, to complete these important tasks for your model of RV, chassis, and power train.

Preventive Maintenance Actions and Tasks

We offer suggestions that you can do yourself for chassis, power train, and coach preventive maintenance. You will probably be relieved to know that most of these tasks are visual checks requiring no tools. All remaining chores can usually be completed with the use of readily available supplies and hand tools of the type that should be carried in the RV.

For our Winnebago Chieftain, which has a Ford 460 V8 engine, the chassis and power train activities were concisely and clearly spelled out in the guide that Winnebago provided for us called the *Ford Motorhome Chassis Service Guide*. It begins with a summary, organized by specific mileage points and time periods, and continues with detailed explanations of each preventive and scheduled maintenance procedure.

Then we discovered that the information describing the services required for the coach and its support systems, appliances, and accessories was scattered between the *Winnebago Chieftain Operator's Manual* and twenty to thirty other documents, each with its own format. We immediately recognized that information was difficult to find and sometimes difficult to understand.

At that point, we started compiling a checklist of appropriate preventive and scheduled service needs using both the coach-supplied documents and the excellent information provided in Bob Livingston's *RV Repair and Maintenance Manual*. We really can't emphasize enough our recommendation that you try Livingston's manual as an excellent source of information for new and experienced RVers. His invaluable guide, complete with preventive and scheduled RV maintenance needs, troubleshooting and repair instructions, and toad towing considerations and requirements, is available from many bookstores and RV supply outlets. Livingston's excellent advice and guidance will help you better understand and maintain your RV.

We've put the preventive maintenance activities below into a checklist format in Appendices B and C for your convenience.

Fluid Levels

Fluid levels should be checked at the start of each trip and at least once a week while you're on the road. This includes checking:

- Brake cylinder
- Power steering reservoir
- Transmission
- Oil
- Radiator (water and antifreeze)
- Windshield washer fluid
- Fresh water tank
- Hydraulic fluid reservoir for leveling and slideout systems

Tire and Wheel Assemblies

The tire and wheel assemblies include the tires, wheel rims, and tire refill hose extender kits. Failure to maintain tire and wheel assemblies exposes you to risk of flat tires and blowouts, which endanger both the RV occupants and the other drivers on the road.

In addition to the information provided in your coach manufacturer documents, we provide the following comments and recommendations for your RV tires and wheels:

- Maintain proper air pressure by checking it at the start of each trip and weekly when in use. The pressure must be checked when the tires are cold. Do not reduce pressure to improve your ride. We carry a high-quality air gauge and an air compressor in our RV at all times. This allows us to conveniently add air at campgrounds, rest stops, on the road, or at home.
- Many RVers use the 120-volt (AC) air compressors because they have more power and fill tires a little faster than the 12-volt (DC) models, but this is a personal and convenience decision. The drawback to 120-volt (AC) compressors is that you might have to start your generator or have an inverter if you are not hooked up to shore power.
- In addition to maintaining the correct air pressure in tires, apply a UV protectant to them monthly. Most tire manufacturers say that the maximum life of a tire is about five years, and that the rays of the sun cause premature

tire damage and weaken tire strength. The regular use of UV protectants will help address these problems of premature damage and weakening.

— If you have decorative stainless wheel liners or covers installed on your wheels, it is important that you make sure they are tight every time you check your air pressure, especially the rear covers. Just tug on them to make sure they are tight. This is important because the air refill extender hoses are usually attached to the wheel liner. If you lose the wheel liner, you will rip the hose out and possibly lose all air pressure in the affected tire. The wheel liners are generally attached to the rim with two nuts that have removable dimpled covers that pull off for access. You will probably need an X-shaped lug wrench or a socket wrench with a 12-inch extension to be able to reach and tighten the retaining nuts on the rear wheels.

— Rotate your tires and align the front end in accordance with the chassis and power train manufacturer schedules. Rotating tires extends the mileage and life of the tires, evens out tire wear, and may reveal problems with the steering and front end. Don't forget to include the spare in the tire rotation activity.

Batteries

Check fluid levels and clean terminals on the engine and coach batteries at the beginning of each trip and monthly while on the road. Use distilled water to bring the water level up to the battery manufacturer—recommended level and a wire brush to clean the terminals. We have noticed that, although the engine battery rarely uses or needs water, the coach batteries use a small amount when out on the road. We found that a battery fill container with a spring-actuated valve and funnel that holds about a quart of water is ideal for adding water to the batteries. We recommend you use a battery hydrometer to check the pH level in your battery cells whenever you service your batteries. These devices are available from auto parts stores.

TV and Satellite Dish Antennas

Lubricate your TV and satellite antennas with silicone spray every three months. Lubricants make it easier to raise, lower, and rotate the antennas, and they also extend the life of the nylon or plastic gear assemblies. Although the replacement parts kits are inexpensive, the labor costs to have a shop repair an antenna, especially a satellite dish, can get expensive.

This task requires going up onto the roof. Have the RV service personnel lubricate the antenna if you have reservations about walking around on top of your RV.

Electric Step

Lubricate the electric step assembly to reduce wear of moving parts and to reduce the load on the electric motor. The owner's manual for the electric step in our Winnebago specifies lubricating all moving parts every thirty days with spray grease. We use Kwik-Lube because the manufacturer specifically says that silicone spray or penetrating oils, such as WD-40, should not be used on step assemblies because the lubricating quality does not last long enough.

In addition to lubricating, check to see that the step retracts when the ignition switch is turned on.

Water System

Check the fresh water tank level at the start of each trip and monitor it during your trips. We recommend draining and refilling your tank if you have not been adding to and using the water in the last thirty days, because the chlorine that is used for purification dissipates over time.

Test the pressure of your accumulator at least quarterly if your RV fresh water system has one. You need an air pressure gauge and compressor or air pump. Most accumulators should be set to 20 PSI, but check the instructions. Change and replace any filter cartridges in the fresh water purification system per the manufacturer instructions and whenever there is a noticeable drop in water pressure.

We recommend an annual routine of checking for loose plumbing fittings, lubricating the toilet flush valve assembly with silicone, and cleaning and disinfecting the fresh water system in accordance with the instructions in your coach manual. The "Groceries and Water" section at the end of

Chapter 5 (Entering Canada and Mexico) explains how to disinfect your fresh water system.

Hot Water Heater

A Lidstone Law of RVing: Only check hot water heaters when they are not in use and when the water is cold.

Hot water heaters in RVs require minimal service. Checking one generally requires opening the outside cover to get access to the tank. Each quarter you should open the relief valve to relieve any pressure that may have built up and reduced the total capacity of the unit. Once a year you should remove the drain plug, drain and flush out the tank, and refill it to remove sediment that may have built up in the bottom of the tank.

If your hot water heater uses anode rods, check the manufacturer instructions for servicing or replacing the rods.

Slideout and Leveling System

Check the fluid level prior to the beginning of a trip and at least monthly. Use the hydraulic or transmission fluid recommended by the manufacturer. You should also remove any accumulated dirt, rocks, mud, ice, or snow from the leveling system jack pistons and feet. Debris might block the complete retraction of the jacks and leave the leveling system warning light and signal energized, or damage the O-ring seals.

We recommend extending the slideout and leveling system every two to three months, even when the RV is not in active use. Many slideout systems use hydraulic pistons, mechanisms, and seals that are lubricated by activating the system. Moving the slideout in and out regularly will also tip you off early to any problems.

Safety Items

We recommend that you check your smoke detectors by pushing the test button before you leave on a trip and weekly when on the road. The 9-volt (DC) smoke detector batteries should be replaced annually. It is also important to test your carbon monoxide detector monthly and to replace the battery annually.

Your RV's LP gas detector should be tested at least quarterly. It is usually wired into the coach's 12-volt (DC) system. The detector sounds an alarm and activates a solenoid that turns off the gas flow when a leak is detected. While many LP detectors turn the gas back on automatically, some have to be manually reset by a button on the gas detector control panel to resume gas flow. We use the gas flow from a butane lighter to test the LP detector in our Winnebago and find that it sets off the alarm in five to ten seconds.

Electrical Systems

Reversed polarity or low voltage can damage the 120-volt (AC) appliances and accessories in your RV. We carry a polarity tester and multimeter. We check the shore power supply the first time we connect it to the RV and again before we turn on any appliances. We also periodically check the voltage level during our stays or whenever we think lights are dimming. There are a number of inexpensive devices to check polarity and voltage and they are readily available from Camping World, most RV supply stores, and RadioShack.

Because we use our generator fairly regularly, we make sure that the oil, oil filter, and air filter are changed after every 100–150 hours of use. We write the date and the accumulated generated hours on the replacement filters when we change them. We also check the spark arrestor every 50 hours.

One of the primary causes of undue wear and tear on RV generators is lack of use. We recommend that you start up your generator every four to six weeks and let it run for ten to twenty minutes when the RV is not in use. Your generator user's manual will tell you how long to run it and how much of a load you should use. At the same time, you can quickly check the refrigerator, microwave, coach air-conditioning system (or furnace, depending on outside temperature), and any other 120-volt (AC) systems or appliances.

Windshield and Wipers

RV windshield wipers are expensive to replace, but there are a couple of things you can easily do to help extend their service life and to ensure good operation when you are driving in inclement weather. For instance, we apply a UV protectant such as 303 or Protect-All to the wiper blades quarterly.

Twice a year, we also apply a rain shield product to the windshield glass and lubricate all moving parts of the wiper assembly (in the engine compartment) with silicone spray or Kwik-Lube. We have found that the rain shield coating helps the wipers to keep the nice big panoramic view through the RV's windshield clear, regardless of the weather.

We strongly recommend that you replace the wiper blades about every two years. If the old ones seem to have some service life remaining, it is a good idea to keep them as a backup either for yourself or for another RVer who badly needs a temporary replacement wiper.

Coach Exterior Sidewall Care and Maintenance

The coach's exterior surfaces include the front and rear caps and sidewalls, and the roof. It's important to keep the exterior clean and protected from UV rays because the sun speeds the fading and deterioration of fiberglass walls and decals. The UV protectant also acts as a semigloss wax. Because our RV lives in Florida, we have to apply UV protectant at least every three to four months. Your coach documents provide specific recommendations for products that will protect the exterior of your RV. Before using a pressure washer (the type used in most truck washes), you should read the cleaning instructions from your coach manufacturer and follow any recommendations, because there may be limitations to or advice on what types of cleaners should be used.

For instance, on our Winnebago, we use a soft brush with a mild soap or detergent to clean the entire RV, including the roof. We then apply UV protectant to the sidewalls, end caps, and roof. There are many excellent protectants, so your selection is a personal choice. If you are not applying UV protectant, then consider using one of the combination car wash/wax solutions available from auto parts stores.

After cleaning and protecting the exterior, you can ensure good operation of the various latch mechanisms on the driver, entrance, and compartment doors by lubricating with silicone spray, 3-in-1 oil, or a suitable powdered graphite lubricant. You should also apply UV protectant to all rubber seals. We do this every four to six months.

Roof Care and Maintenance

Roof maintenance and care requires a visit to the roof of your RV. If you are reluctant or unable to climb up and walk around your roof, have an RV service shop do the cleaning and detailing. Some RV shops that do cleaning and detailing do not include prepping the roof, so you may have to discuss extra costs with the service manager or find another service provider.

Your RV roof will wear better if you use the specific cleaners and protectants recommended by the RV maker. A combination of dust, road dirt, leaves, mildew, and bird droppings will accumulate on your RV's roof. Accumulation is not only unsightly, but can cause discoloration that is difficult to remove. Since our Winnebago has a fiberglass roof, we clean and protect it with the same products we use for the sidewalls and end caps.

Rubber roofs need different care than fiberglass, aluminum, or metal roofs. Before scrubbing away on the RV's roof or setting someone else to the job, you should review your coach documents to determine the appropriate products and steps for cleaning and protecting it. The cleaners necessary to remove mildew from a rubber roof are very strong, so special steps and precautions are required to prevent damaging the roof or discoloring the sidewalls. We recommend you consult with an RV service professional if the rubber membrane on your RV shows heavy mildew or cracking. We also recommend you apply UV protectant to the rubber at least twice a year.

While up on the roof, you will probably find it convenient to lubricate the TV and satellite antennas, check the roof vents for blockage, and check the air-conditioning shrouds for leaves and dirt. Finally, check all seams to make sure that the various joints and items attached to or through the roof are properly sealed and watertight.

Your coach documentation provides a specific list of the various sealants used on your RV. For example, our Winnebago uses five different types, but all are inexpensive and readily available from the dealer and RV service shops. Do not use silicone caulking on your RV because it retains moisture.

If you are paying RV service personnel to clean the roof, you might want to have them lubricate the antennas, clean out the air-conditioner shrouds, and perform any other necessary roof-related cleaning and servicing.

Awnings

Awnings should be cleaned every time you clean the RV. We begin by washing the awning with the same mild soap or detergent we use to wash the RV. We then clean the awning with a mixture of $\frac{1}{4}$ cup liquid soap, $\frac{1}{4}$ cup bleach, and 5 gallons of warm water. Be sure to clean the top and bottom of the awning and rinse both sides of the awning thoroughly. It should be left extended until completely dry.

After cleaning the awning, we apply a silicone spray lubricant to all parts that slide out or move. You should check all awning attachment brackets for tightness with a socket wrench or adjustable wrench at least once a year.

We recommend that you refer all service or repairs needed on the awning's spring assembly to professional RV service shops. This awning spring is under very high tension and can cause extensive injury to you and to the RV if the assembly comes apart without warning.

Coach Air-Conditioning System

Most RVs have external single or dual roof-mounted units for the compressor section and internal vents or plenum systems to distribute the cooled air to the RV interior. User maintenance consists primarily of cleaning the interior filter weekly while on the road and cleaning out any accumulated debris and leaves from the external shroud assembly annually. When the shroud cover is removed with a screwdriver to clean out debris, you should use a socket wrench or adjustable wrench to check that the mounting nuts securing the compressor assembly to the roof are tight.

You should start up the air-conditioning system every six to eight weeks during periods when the RV is parked and not in use. Wait until a day when the outside air temperature is hot enough to allow you to verify that the air-conditioning has kicked in, or run a heater or furnace inside the RV to raise the temperature.

Furnace, Stove, and Refrigerator

RVers should start up furnaces, stoves, and refrigerators every six to eight weeks when the RV is not in active use. Outside vents for these appliances should be visually checked to make sure they are not blocked. If they are blocked, carefully remove leaves and debris manually. If a wasp or bees' nest has been built in the vent, check to see if the residents are at home. If the nest is occupied, you will probably have to very carefully terminate their residence by chemical means.

Authorized dealers or professional RV shops should service your furnace, stove, and refrigerator once a year. Find a provider who will (in accordance with the manufacturer recommendations) check for LP pressure, correct flame height, proper airflow, and other factors.

Scheduled and Major Maintenance Needs

This section addresses the scheduled maintenance activities for your RV, including both the coach servicing requirements and those of your chassis and power train. Scheduling maintenance service for your coach's chassis and power train is the most important action you can take to make sure your RV is always ready and able to go. And, more importantly, keeping up on scheduled and major maintenance checks will guarantee that you won't void your RV's warranty conditions.

We strongly recommend that you use authorized dealers that have good reputations within the community and come recommended by other RVers, because scheduled and major maintenance checks are complicated and require elaborate procedures, special tools, and safety precautions. Authorized dealers have the knowledge and trained service personnel, as well as factory support, to complete these important tasks for your model of RV, chassis, and power train. We use a Ford heavy-truck dealer for the power train and chassis needs, and our Winnebago dealer for the coach systems.

The technical and service documents provided by RV, associated equipment, and chassis and power train manufacturers provide extensive information describing specific required maintenance and service actions and when they should be performed. Also, you can certainly discuss your maintenance schedule and activities at any time with your RV service shop personnel to become as informed as possible.

Coach and Related Systems Maintenance

Some tasks for maintenance of coach systems and accessories that require professional attention are:

- Major generator service, including removing and servicing cylinder heads
- Cleaning and checking the refrigerator burner assembly and flue
- Cleaning, checking, and servicing the furnace
- Cleaning and servicing the hot water heater
- Servicing and repairing leveling and slideout systems
- Installation, removal, and repair of awning assemblies
- Roof repairs

These are critical maintenance procedures for expensive RV components and must be done correctly.

Chassis and Power Train Maintenance

Scheduled chassis and power train maintenance consists of such tasks as:

- Changing fluids and filters
- Checking fluid levels and belts
- Checking major systems for proper operation, defects, and wear
- Rotating and balancing tires
- Aligning front end

Most gas-powered motorhomes, including our gas-powered Winnebago Chieftain, require chassis and power train maintenance every 3,000 miles. The time that should elapse between service appointments varies according to the chassis manufacturer requirements. Diesel power plants are much more complex and require different types of services and service frequencies. However, all chassis and power train maintenance service needs are clearly spelled out in the service guide included in the technical documentation for your motorhome.

In addition to the scheduled chassis and power train maintenance tasks described above, there are also "major" chassis and power train maintenance items that are necessary. These might include, but are not limited to, the following items:

- Hydraulic or air brake service
- Transmission service
- Rear axle service
- Power plant tune-up
- Cooling system service

A Lidstone Law of RVing: Protect your safety and the terms of your RV's warranty by diligently staying up-to-date on effective preventive and scheduled maintenance procedures.

Together, the scheduled and major chassis and power train maintenances are critically important because they allow the RV owner to obtain the maximum service life from the engine, transmission, brake system, and related power train, steering, and suspension.

CHAPTER 18

STORING THE RV OVER THE WINTER

After that long, housebound winter, you will want to be able to jump in your RV at the first ray of warm sunshine and get on the road for a trip to a new and exciting destination. If you follow the advice in this chapter, your RV will be in great condition and ready to hit the road on March 21, when the vernal equinox signals the start of spring in the Northern Hemisphere. We talk here about how to store your RV over the winter in such a way that low temperatures and inclement weather will not damage it. We covered some of these guidelines in Chapter 14 (Returning Home), so you are probably already well versed on some winter-prep tasks.

We strongly urge you to review both your coach and your chassis and power train manuals. These documents include extensive and well-written information explaining the activities that are necessary to put your RV into a winterized mode and how to get it back on the road in the spring.

Most RVers think of protecting the fresh water system, hot water heater, and holding tanks as the primary required winterization activities. However, this is also an excellent time to make sure that all preventive and scheduled service needs are completed, as this will get you back on the road much faster in the spring.

Don't forget to remove any liquid products from the RV interior and storage bays that could be damaged by freezing or cause damage if they leak or rupture as a result of freezing. We also recommend you remove high-value or portable items subject to theft.

We recommend that RVers complete a combination of housekeeping and maintenance activities on the following systems:

- Engine and power train
- Coach
- Fresh water system and hot water system
- Holding tanks

Although the RVer will attend to the housekeeping actions, all other winterizing tasks can be done either by the RVer or by an experienced RV service shop. (RVers in Alaska and other cold states, where temperatures are close to or below freezing in the spring and fall, should plan for maintenance as needed.)

If you plan on having RV maintenance work done on the engine and power train or on the coach, consider having the winterization of the fresh water system (and possibly the holding tanks) performed by the RV service shop as well. The cost will be in the $50–$150 range depending on the number of components that require service.

Engine and Power Train

- Have any needed RV service completed (e.g., lube and oil, repairs, etc.).
- Add the appropriate fuel stabilizer to gas-powered RVs. This will prevent mold from forming in diesel fuel and it will prevent gasoline from deteriorating.
- Ensure that diesel-powered RVs have the proper fuel and fuel stabilizers for winter use. (If you run the engine in very cold weather, the wrong fuel may cause problems.)
- Ensure that the engine cooling system has sufficient quality and level of coolant to prevent freezing. (Remember that the coolant has to be replaced periodically per your chassis and power train maintenance schedule to prevent damage to the radiator.)

Coach

- Perform required preventive maintenance—see Chapter 17 (Preventive Maintenance).
- Clean the interior and exterior of the RV.
- Check, clean, and reorganize the contents of all interior cabinets and all exterior storage bays.
- Fill the propane tank and turn the valve off.
- Remove all food items.

— If security is a possible problem, remove clothing, personal items, and support items.

— Empty and clean the refrigerator and freezer. Make sure the doors are left partially open.

— Close shades and drapes to reduce UV damage to upholstery and carpeting from sunlight.

— Open the roof vents slightly to allow fresh air into the RV and prevent mildew.

— Actuate the coach battery disconnect feature (if you have one) or disconnect the positive lead to prevent the batteries from being drained by the LP gas detector, electric clocks, and other 12-volt (DC) devices.

— Ensure that the tires are inflated to the correct pressure (tires tend to have a slight drop over long periods).

— Slide a small block under the wiper blades to raise them off the windshield and keep them from sticking to the windshield.

— Put on the RV cover to protect finish and wheel covers to protect tires.

To lift the weight of the RV off the tires during the winter, consider raising the RV with the leveling jacks or air bags. We advise that you put compatible jack stands under the chassis and then raise the leveling jacks or deflate the air bags as appropriate.

A Lidstone Law of RVing: Never leave the RV resting on lowered leveling jacks or inflated air bags during the storage period or for any other extended time period.

We recommend placing jack stands under the RV and deactivating the leveling system when leaving the RV in one place for more than three or four weeks.

If you do leave your jacks extended, we recommend putting a light coat of grease on the exposed pistons to reduce rust or pitting and to protect the O rings. In addition, the hydraulic fluid level for the RV slideout and jacks should be checked as a preventive maintenance task before you extend or raise them. A lower than recommended level might indicate a leak.

Fresh Water System

The fresh water system varies based on the RV model, but may include the following components:

- Fresh water holding tank
- Outside shower
- Hot water heater
- Kitchen and bath sinks
- Shower
- Toilet
- Water filtration system
- Ice maker
- Dryer/washing machine

As part of your winterizing maintenance procedures, you can prevent damage to these components in two ways: you can simply drain and clear the water lines, or you can first drain and clear the water lines and then add RV antifreeze. Either procedure prevents damage to parts caused by freezing.

Regardless of which method you choose, begin by completely draining all fresh water from the fresh water holding tank and distribution system. Open all the faucets while draining to prevent a vacuum from retaining some water in the lines. Then blow compressed air through the entire system to make sure that all lines are cleared. The full fresh water system includes the fresh water holding tank, water pump, all plumbing lines, fixtures (e.g., faucets, shower, outside shower), and hot water heater. The fresh water system also includes any installed water filtration system, ice maker, and washing machine hookup.

A Lidstone Law of RVing: Always level the RV before you begin draining the fresh water system. Your RV coach documents will tell you where to locate petcocks and drains, which must respectively be opened and drained.

Follow the instructions in your RV documents or maintenance manuals for using compressed air to clear the lines. Your technical documents for the hot water heater, water filtration system, ice maker, and washing machine hookups spell out the specific steps in detail for winterizing these accessories. If you do not have the applicable coach and appliance documents, refer to Bob Livingston's *RV Repair and Maintenance Manual.*

Special Considerations for Adding RV Antifreeze

You will spend less on antifreeze if you drain the entire system first. Then, pump RV fresh water system antifreeze through all the lines. You can obtain this type of antifreeze from RV suppliers.

A Lidstone Law of RVing: Poisonous chemicals are used in the manufacturing of standard automotive antifreeze. Never use standard automotive antifreeze to winterize an RV's fresh water system.

You should refer to your specific coach documents to locate the procedure required to add antifreeze to the water system and related accessories. The recommended procedure is to add it using the inlet side of the water pump. Go inside the RV and open one faucet. This action starts the pump, which draws the antifreeze out of its container, through the pump, and into the fresh water plumbing lines. Keep the pump running until antifreeze runs out of the faucet. Do the same with each faucet, including those in the shower or bathtub. Flush the toilet until it starts to fill with antifreeze. Finally, pour a cup of RV antifreeze into each drain.

When getting ready to travel again the next season, you will have to remove all traces of antifreeze from the system. Do so by following the same faucets/shower/toilet flushing procedure described above. However, first you must hook up to a water line or fill the RV's fresh water tank so that you can run fresh water through the RV's components.

When you make sure that all winterizing procedures described in your RV's documents are followed to the letter; you protect your fresh water system from expensive damage. You should also be sure to follow manufacturer instructions for draining and adding antifreeze. Freezing weather can cause damage to water heaters, water filtration systems, and ice makers because water system components can retain enough water to rupture pipes and cause other damage.

Holding Tanks

— Flush the toilet and make sure the bowl is empty.

— Drain the black and gray water holding tanks.

— Rinse the black water holding tank if you have a flushing system.

— Check that the holding tanks are empty.

— If you added antifreeze to the fresh water system, put a small amount in the gray water and black water holding tanks per instructions.

— If you do not add antifreeze to the drained gray water and black water holding tanks, leave the dump valves open, and remove the dust cover from the holding tank outlet.

— If you removed the dust cover from the holding tank outlet, be sure to hang a tag on the steering wheel stating the dump valve needs to be closed and the dust cover secured prior to moving or using the RV.

Note: Opening the dump valve and removing the dust cover help to vent the holding tanks and reduce the amount of odors entering the RV.

State Park Websites and Related Information

The websites in this section were found by using an internet search engine (www.metacrawler.com) and entering the state name followed by the phrase "state parks" (e.g., "Alaska state parks," "Washington state parks," etc.). The information below is compiled from the top websites found in each search.

Many of the states also have tourism information websites that provide a great deal of miscellaneous information, although they may or may not include the state parks and forests. The tourism websites are listed in the major campground directories.

Because website names and addresses tend to change over time, you may have to check for updated information using an internet search engine.

Alabama

Division of State Parks

Alabama Department of Conservation and Natural Resources

64 N. Union St.

Montgomery, AL 36130

1-800-ALA-PARK (Information)

www.state.al.us

Comments: Click on "Alabama State Parks"; links to 24 state parks.

Alaska

DNR Public Information Center

550 W. Seventh Ave., Suite 1260

Anchorage, AK 99501

1-907-269-8400 (Information)

www.dced.state.ak.us/tourism

Comments: Select "Attractions and Activities," click on "State Parks"; contains information on state and national parks; no reservations—campsites available on first-come, first-served basis.

ARIZONA

Arizona State Parks

1300 Washington

Phoenix, AZ 85007

1-602-542-4174 (Information)

www.arizonaguide.com

Comments: Click on "Things to See," click on "Outdoor AZ," then click on "Camping"; all campsites available on first-come, first-served basis; includes links to national parks and monuments.

ARKANSAS

Arkansas Department of Parks and Tourism

One Capitol Mall

Little Rock, AR 72201

1-888-AT-PARKS (Information)

www.arkansas.com

Comments: Click on "State Parks"; contact individual state parks to make reservations.

CALIFORNIA

California Department of Parks and Recreation

P.O. Box 942896

Sacramento, CA 94296

1-800-444-PARK (Reservations)

1-800-274-7275 (TDD Reservations)

www.cal-parks.ca.gov

Comments: Provides links to 269 state parks and properties.

COLORADO

Colorado State Parks

1313 Sherman St., #618

Denver, CO 80203

1-800-678-2267 (Reservations)

www.parks.state.co.us

Comments: "Fun finder" helps select parks based on location, recreation, elevation, and facility needs.

CONNECTICUT
State Parks Division, Bureau of Outdoor Recreation DEP
79 Elm St.
Hartford, CT 06106
1-877-668-CAMP
www.dep.state.ct.us/rec/parks.htm
Comments: Click on "Camping," then click on "Camping in Connecticut."

DELAWARE
Division of Parks and Recreation
89 Kings Highway
Dover, DE 19901
1-877-98-PARKS (Reservations)
www.destateparks.com
Comments: Click on "Things to Do," then click on "Camping."

FLORIDA
Department of Environmental Protection
Division of Recreation and Parks
3900 Commonwealth Blvd.
Tallahassee, FL 32399
1-850-488-9872 (Information)
www.myflorida.com
Comments: Click on "Florida Recreation and Parks"; provides phone numbers, addresses, and links to individual state parks and private RV parks and campgrounds.

GEORGIA
Georgia State Parks
205 Butler St., Suite 1354 East
Atlanta, GA 30334

1-800-864-7275 (Reservations)

www.gastateparks.org

Comments: Click on "Accommodations and Rates"; links to conservation, tourist, and National Forest Service websites.

IDAHO

Idaho State Parks and Recreation

P.O. Box 83270

Boise, ID 83270-0065

1-208-334-4199 (Information)

www.idahoparks.org

Comments: Gives individual state park phone numbers for reservations; includes 27 state parks, national parks, and Idaho BLM lands.

ILLINOIS

Illinois Department of Natural Resources

Division of Land Management

524 S. Second St.

Springfield, IL 62701

1-217-782-6752 (Information)

www.dnr.state.il.us/lands/landmgt/parks

Comments: Reservations can be made by mail or in person at individual state parks; telephone reservations accepted at specific sites.

INDIANA

Division of State Parks and Reservoirs

204 W. Washington St., Room W298

Indianapolis, IN 46204

1-317-232-4124 (Information)

www.state.in.us/dnr

Comments: Click on "State Parks and Reservoirs," then click on "Camping"; reservations can be mailed to selected state parks; includes links to public (municipal, county, and federal) campgrounds, private RV parks and campgrounds, ski resorts, golf courses, etc.

IOWA

Parks, Recreation and Preserves Division

Iowa Department of Natural Resources

Wallace State Office Bldg.

502 E. Bank St.

Des Moines, IA 50319

1-515-281-5918

www.state.ia.us/dnr

    Comments: Click on "Parks/Recreation/Preserves"; lists individual parks, addresses, and phone numbers; reservations not accepted.

KANSAS

Kansas Department of Wildlife and Parks

512 SE 25th Ave.

Pratt, KS 67124

1-316-672-5911 (Information)

www.kdwp.state.ks.us/parks/parks.html

    Comments: Make reservations at individual state parks in person, by mail, or by phone.

KENTUCKY

Kentucky Department of Parks

Capital Plaza Tower

500 Mero St., Suite 1100

Frankfort, KY 40601

1-800-255-PARK (allows toll-free connections to individual state parks)

www.kytourism.com

    Comments: Click on "Nations Finest Parks"; links to 49 state parks.

LOUISIANA

Office of State Parks

P.O. Box 44426

Baton Rouge, LA 70804

1-877-CAMP-N-LA (Reservations)

1-888-677-1400 (Information)

www.crt.state.la.us

>   *Comments:* Click on "State Parks."

MAINE

Department of Conservation

Bureau of Parks and Lands

22 State House Station

Augusta, ME 04333

1-800-332-1501 (Reservations from outside Maine)

1-207-287-3824 (Reservations from inside Maine)

www.state.me.us/doc/parks

>   *Comments:* Click on "Camping."

MARYLAND

Maryland Department of Natural Resources

State Forest and Park Service

580 Taylor Ave., E-3

Annapolis, MD 21401

1-888-432-2267 (Reservations)

www.dnr.state.md.us/publiclands

>   *Comments:* Click on "Maryland's Parks, Forests, and WMAs"; links to state parks by region.

MASSACHUSETTS

Department of Environmental Management

251 Causeway St., Suite 600

Boston, MA 02114

1-877-I-CAMP-MA (Reservations)

www.state.ma.us/dem/recreate/camping.htm

>   *Comments:* 28 campgrounds available within state forests and parks.

MICHIGAN

Michigan Parks and Recreation Bureau

530 W. Allegan St.

Lansing, MI 48933

1-800-44-PARKS (Reservations)

1-517-373-9900 (Information)

www.dnr.state.mi.us

    Comments: Click on "Camping"; includes listings of 96 state parks.

MINNESOTA

DNR Information Center

500 Lafayette Rd.

St. Paul, MN 55155

1-800-246-CAMP or 1-952-922-9000 (Reservations)

1-800-MINNDNR or 1-651-296-6157 (Information)

www.dnr.state.mn.us

    Comments: Click on "State Parks" or "State Forests."

MISSISSIPPI

Mississippi Department of Wildlife, Fisheries and Parks

1505 Eastover Dr.

Jackson, MS 39211

1-800-GO-PARKS (Information)

www.mdwfp.com

    Comments: Click on "Parks"; contact individual state parks for reservations.

MISSOURI

Department of Natural Resources

Division of State Parks

P.O. Box 176

Johnson City, MO 65102

1-800-334-6946 (Reservations)

www.mostateparks.com

    Comments: Click on "Camping" for reservation information.

MONTANA

Montana Fish, Wildlife and Parks

P.O. Box 200701

Helena, MT 59620

1-406-444-2535 (Information)

www.fwp.state.mt.us

    Comments: Click on "Parks"; make reservations via individual state park phone numbers.

NEBRASKA

Nebraska Game and Parks Commission

2200 N. 33rd St.

Lincoln, NE 68053

1-800-228-4307 (Information)

http://ngp.ngpc.state.ne.us/gp.html

    Comments: Click on "Parks and Rec"; reservations accepted at specific parks, all others available on first-come, first-served basis.

NEVADA

Nevada Division of State Parks

1300 S. Curry St.

Carson City, NV 89703

1-775-687-4384 (Information)

www.state.nv.us/stparks

    Comments: Provides information on 24 state parks.

NEW HAMPSHIRE

N.H. Division of Parks and Recreation

172 Pembroke Rd., P.O. Box 1856

Concord, NH 03302

1-603-271-3556 (Information)

www.worknplaynhusa.com/index.html

    Comments: Click on "State Parks"; lots of miscellaneous links.

NEW JERSEY

New Jersey Department of Environmental Protection

Division of Parks and Forestry

501 E. State St., P.O. Box 404

Trenton, NJ 08625

1-800-843-6420 (Information)

www.nj.com/outdoors/parks.html

   Comments: Click on any park to get to all activities offered; make reservations via individual state park phone numbers.

NEW MEXICO

New Mexico State Parks Division

P.O. Box 1147

Santa Fe, NM 87504

1-877-NM-4-RSVP (Reservations)

1-888-NMPARKS (Information)

www.emnrd.state.nm.us

   Comments: Click on "State Parks Division"; 31 state parks; lots of miscellaneous links.

NEW YORK

New York State OPRHP

Public Affairs, 13th Floor, Agency Bldg.

Empire State Plaza

Albany, NY 12238

1-800-456-2267 (Reservations)

1-518-474-0456 (Information)

www.nysparks.state.ny.us

   Comments: Click on "Explore Here."

North Carolina

North Carolina State Parks

512 N. Salisbury St., Archdale Bldg., 7th Floor, Room 732

Raleigh, NC 27699

1-919-733-4181 (Information)

www.ils.unc.edu/parkproject

Comments: Most sites available on first-come, first-served basis; reservations can be made at three state parks by contacting them directly by phone.

North Dakota

North Dakota Parks and Recreation Department

1835 Bismarck Expressway

Bismarck, ND 58504

1-800-807-4723 (Reservations)

1-701-328-5357 (Information)

www.state.nd.us/ndparks

Comments: Includes information on 16 state parks.

Ohio

Ohio Department of Natural Resources

Division of Parks and Recreation

1952 Belcher Dr., C-3

Columbus, OH 43224

1-614-265-6513 (Information)

www.dnr.state.oh.us

Comments: Click on "State Parks and Resorts"; sites available on first-come, first-served basis; 46 parks allow "Call-Ahead Registration" on the day of arrival.

OKLAHOMA

Oklahoma Department of Tourism

15 N. Robinson St., 8th Floor

Oklahoma City, OK 73102

1-800-654-8240 (Reservations and Information)

http://www.touroklahoma.com

Comments: Click on "State Parks"; includes information on 16 state parks.

OREGON

Oregon State Parks

P.O. Box 500

Portland, OR 97207

1-800-452-5687 (Reservations)

1-800-551-6949 (Information)

www.prd.state.or.us

Comments: Half of the state parks operate on first-come, first-served basis, although reservations are available at the other parks.

PENNSYLVANIA

Bureau of State Parks

P.O. Box 8551

Harrisburg, PA 17105

1-888-PA-PARKS (Reservations and Information)

www.dcnr.state.pa.us

Comments: Click on "Outdoor Adventures," then click on "State Parks"; includes information on 116 state parks.

RHODE ISLAND

Division of Parks and Recreation

2321 Hartford Ave.

Johnston, RI 02919

1-401-222-2632 (Information)

www.riparks.com

Comments: Click on "Recreation Map"; make reservations directly with individual parks.

SOUTH CAROLINA

South Carolina Department of Parks, Recreation, and Tourism

P.O. Box 71

Columbia, SC 29202

1-803-734-0122 (Information)

www.southcarolinaparks.com

Comments: Make reservations via individual state park phone numbers; links to state parks, national parks, and tourism sites.

SOUTH DAKOTA

SD State Parks

523 E. Capitol Ave.

Pierre, SD 57501

1-800-710-CAMP (Reservations)

1-605-773-3391 (Information)

www.state.sd.us/gfp

Comments: Click on "Parks"; includes links to many other state parks and agencies in the United States.

TENNESSEE

Tennessee Department of Environment and Conservation

State Parks and Recreation

401 Church St.

Nashville, TN 37243

1-800-GO-2-TENN (Reservations)

www.state.tn.us

Comments: Click on "Travel and Recreation," then click on "State Parks and Outdoors," then click on "State Parks"; most campgrounds available on first-come, first-served basis only.

TEXAS

Texas Parks and Wildlife

4200 Smith School Rd.

Austin, TX 78744

1-512-389-8900 (Reservations)

1-800-792-1112 (Information)

www.tpwd.state.tx.us

> *Comments*: Click on "Parks"; links to state and national parks in Texas.

UTAH

Utah Department of Natural Resources

Division of Parks and Recreation

1594 West North Temple

Salt Lake City, UT 84114

1-800-322-3770 (Reservations)

1-801-538-7220 (Information)

http://parks.state.ut.us

> *Comments*: Click on "State Parks."

VERMONT

Vermont Parks Department

103 S. Main St., 10 South

Waterbury, VT 05671

1-802-241-3655 (Information)

www.vtstateparks.com

> *Comments*: Click on "Find a Park"; reservations accepted through state parks regional offices.

VIRGINIA

Department of Conservation and Recreation

203 Governor St., Suite 213

Richmond, VA 23219

1-800-933-PARK

www.state.va.us/dcr

Comments: Click on "State Parks"; campgrounds provided in 22 state parks.

WASHINGTON

Washington State Parks and Recreation Commission

P.O. Box 42650

Olympia, WA 98504

1-800-452-5687 (Reservations)

1-800-233-0321 (Information)

www.parks.wa.gov

> *Comments*: Gives information on 125 state parks.

WEST VIRGINIA

West Virginia Department of Natural Resources

Parks and Recreation Section

State Capitol, Bldg. 3, Room 713

Charleston, WV 25305

1-800-CALL-WVA (Information)

www.wvparks.com

> *Comments*: Reservations accepted at select campgrounds.

WISCONSIN

Wisconsin Department of Natural Resources

Parks and Recreation

P.O. Box 7921

Madison, WI 53707

1-888-WI-PARKS (Reservations)

1-608-266-2181 (Information)

www.dnr.state.wi.us/org/land/parks

> *Comments*: Lists information for 85 state parks and trails; some campsites available on first-come, first-served basis only.

WYOMING

Division of State Parks and Historic Sites

122 W. 25th St., Herschler Bldg., First Floor East

Cheyenne, WY 82002

1-307-777-6323 (Information)

http://spacr.state.wy.us/sphs

Comments: No reservations—campsites available on first-come, first-served basis only.

SUGGESTED CHASSIS AND POWER TRAIN PREVENTIVE MAINTENANCE CHECKLIST

Item	Maintenance Action	Frequency	Supplies and Tools
Fluid Levels	Check fluid level in brake cylinder	At start of trip and weekly when in use	
	Check fluid level in power steering and transmission	At start of trip and weekly when in use	
	Check oil level	At start of trip and weekly when in use	
	Check radiator and windshield washer levels	At start of trip and weekly when in use	
Tires	Maintain correct air pressure	At start of trip and weekly when in use	Air pressure gauge and compressor
	Rotate tires	Per chassis manufacturer instructions	
	UV protectant	Monthly	303 Protectorant or Protect-All
Wheel Liners and Tire Refill Extenders	Check for tightness by tugging on wheel liner	Every time air pressure is checked	Socket wrench and extension (and pliers if loose)
Engine Battery	Check fluid levels and clean terminals	At start of trip and monthly	Distilled water and wire brush

– – – – – –

SUGGESTED COACH-RELATED PREVENTIVE MAINTENANCE CHECKLIST

Item	Maintenance Action	Frequency	Supplies and Tools
TV Antenna	Lubricate	Quarterly	Silicone spray
Manual Satellite Antenna	Lubricate	Quarterly	Silicone spray
Electrical or Manual Step	Lubricate	Quarterly	Kwik-Lube
Fluid Levels	Check fresh water tank level	At start of trip and weekly when in use	Water
	Check hydraulic fluid reservoir level for slideout and leveling system	At start of trip and weekly when in use	Hydraulic fluid
Water System:			
Toilet	Lubricate flush valve	Annually	Silicone spray
	Check tightness of fittings	Annually	Adjustable wrench
Fresh Water Tank	Drain and refill	At the start of each trip	
Fresh Water Tank and Plumbing System	Clean and disinfect	Annually	Household chlorine bleach
Accumulator	Maintain air pressure @ 20 PSI	Quarterly	Air pressure gauge and compressor
Water Filter	Replace	Annually or when flow decreases	Filter cartridge
Hot Water Heater	Drain, flush, and refill	Annually	
	Open relief valve	Quarterly	

Item	Maintenance Action	Frequency	Supplies and Tools
Slideout and Jacks	Check fluid levels, pH levels, and clean terminals	Quarterly	Transmission fluid, battery hydrometer, distilled water, and wire brush
	Clean dirt and mud from jacks	As required	
Safety Items:			
Smoke Detector	Test	Weekly when RV is in use	
	Replace battery	Annually	9V battery
CO Detector	Test	Monthly	
	Replace battery	Annually	9V battery
LP Detector	Test	Quarterly	Use gas flow from unlit butane lighter
Electrical Systems:			
120V (AC)	Check polarity and voltage	At every campground hookup	Polarity tester and voltmeter or multitester
Generator	Check spark arrestor	Every 50 hours	
	Change oil and filter	Every 100–150 hours	Generator oil and oil filter
	Change air filter	Every 100–150 hours	Air filter cartridge
Coach Batteries	Check fluid levels, pH levels, and clean terminals	At start of trip and monthly	Battery hydrometer, distilled water, and wire brush
Windshield	Apply UV protectant to wipers	Quarterly	303 Protectorant or Protect-All
	Apply rain shield to windshield	Semiannually	Rain shield and squeegee

Item	Maintenance Action	Frequency	Supplies and Tools
Windshield (*cont.*)	Lubricate wiper mechanism	Semiannually	Silicone spray
	Replace wipers	When streaking occurs or every 2 years	Wiper blades
RV Front and Rear Cap and Sidewalls	Wash, wax, apply UV protectant	3–4 times per year	Protect-All
Roof	Wash and prepare roof surface	3–4 times per year per manufacturer recommendations	
	Check for potential or actual leaks	Annually	Manufacturer-recommended sealants
Doors—Entrance, Driver, and Compartments	Lubricate latch mechanisms	Semiannually	Silicone spray
	Apply UV protectant to rubber seals	Semiannually	303 Protectorant or Protect-All
Awning	Remove dirt and mildew	Semiannually	Liquid soap and bleach per manufacturer instructions
Air-Conditioning:			
Interior Filters	Clean with water	Weekly when in use	
External Shroud	Clean out debris and leaves	Annually	Screwdriver
Rooftop Unit	Check for tightness	Annually	Screwdriver and socket wrenches
Furnace	Check exhaust for soot	Weekly when in use	Existence of soot requires service by authorized dealer

SAMPLE CHECKLIST FOR LOADING RV

Clothing and Personal	Bathroom	Kitchen	Kitchen
___ Underwear	___ Prescriptions	___ Ice trays	___ Coffee
___ Socks	___ Vitamins	___ Ice (for cooler)	___ Coffee filters
___ Sneakers	___ Tub bathmat	___ Freezer packs	___ Pretzels
___ Shoes	___ Toothbrush	___ Cheese grater	___ Peanut butter
___ Hiking boots	___ Toothpaste	___ Cleanser	___ Marmalade
___ Jewelry	___ Floss	___ Glass cleaner	___ Cereal
___ Earplugs	___ Pick/scraper	___ Paper towels	___ Foil
___ Sweaters	___ Shaving kit	___ Liquid detergent	___ Plastic wrap
___ Perfume	___ Makeup	___ Bleach	___ Plastic bags
___ Shorts	___ Cotton pads	___ Softener	___ Cream cheese
___ Pants	___ Q-tips	___ Dish detergent	___ Milk
___ Sleeveless shirts	___ Shampoo	___ Cookbooks	___ Sugar
___ Outdoor coats	___ Conditioner	___ Scrubbies	___ Fresh fruit
___ Turtlenecks	___ Bug repellent	___ Cooking	___ Spray oil
___ Denim skirt	___ Peroxide	thermometer	___ Bagels
___ Jackets	___ Band-Aids	___ Can opener	___ Margarine
___ Sports and	___ Betadine	___ Tuna fish	___ Soft drinks
knit shirts	___ Cortisone	___ Mayonnaise	___ Crackers
___ Khakis	___ Antibiotic	___ Mustard	___ Spaghetti
___ Slacks	ointment	___ Ketchup	and sauce
	___ Nail-polish	___ Knives	___ Graham crackers
	remover	___ Soups	___ Cookies
	___ Nail files	___ Bottled water	___ Water bottles
	___ Hair dryer	___ Wine	___ Eggs
	___ Hair spray	___ Liquor	___ Canned fruit
	___ Hair rollers		___ Juice
	___ Towelettes		___ Condiments
	___ Towels		
	___ Wash cloths		

Miscellaneous	Garage	Den	Office
___ Heating pads	___ Beach bags	___ Kids' toys	___ Address book
___ Exercise pad	___ Beach chairs	___ Sewing supplies	___ TV and remote
___ Sheets	___ Golf clubs	___ Embroidery	___ Work materials
___ Pillow cases	___ Golf balls	___ Knitting	___ Markers
___ Pillows	___ Socket set	___ Phonebooks	___ Pens and pencils
___ Extra eyeglasses	___ Electric	___ Trailer Life	___ Envelopes
___ Sunglasses	screwdriver	directory	___ Packing tape
___ Hats	___ Power drill and	___ Woodall's	___ Scissors
___ Umbrellas	attachments	directory	___ Writing pads
___ Sunblock	___ Citronella	___ RV manual	___ Checkbook
___ Camera	candles	___ Travel guides	___ Outstanding bills
___ Film	___ Electric cooler	___ RV repair manual	___ List of bills
___ Purse	___ Wood blocks	___ Exit/truck stop	payable and
___ Wallets	(jacks)	guides	labels
___ Fanny pack	___ RV UV/polish	___ RV Trip Book	___ Stamps
___ ATM/debit cards	___ Small cooler	and bag	___ Cellular phone
___ Money	___ Shoe-shine kit		___ Diskettes
___ Travelers checks	___ Glue		___ Tape
___ Credit cards	___ Air compressor		___ Stapler
	___ Voltmeter		___ Laptop computer
	___ Tank chemicals		___ Keyboard
	___ Folding tables		___ Serial mouse
	___ Bucket and brush		___ Computer
			software CDs
			___ HMO provider
			list
			___ Dental provider
			list

INDEX

AAA, 139; road service, 168
AAA CampBooks, 15
AAA Map'n'Go, 141, 143
Air-conditioning; preventive maintenance, 190; preventive maintenance checklist, 218
Anderson's Campground and RV Park Travel Directory, 15
Antifreeze, 68
Awnings, 59; preventive maintenance, 190; setup, 158

Banking and money, 104; ATM/debit cards, 105, 106–107; bill paying (automated), 110; bill paying by check, 109–110; bill paying by EFT or card, 111; bill paying options, 108; Canada, 78–79; cash, 104, 106; credit cards, 107–108; electronic funds transfer, 105; internet, 105; Mexico, 82; overdraft protection, 106; regional or national banks, 105, 106
Battery maintenance, 184

Campgrounds; county, 34; directories and guides, 15–16; private memberships, 19–21; websites, 27–28
Camping Life, 21
Camping World, 21, 168
Canada, 77; gas and diesel fuel, 78; groceries, 79; guns, 78; insurance, 78; money exchange, 78–79; pets, 78; TV, 79
Chassis; extended warranty, 171; manuals and documents, 176; preventive maintenance checklist, 215; scheduled maintenance, 192–193; scheduled service, 86, 87–88; warranty, 169–170
Coach; extended warranty, 171; exterior sidewall maintenance, 188; preventive maintenance checklist, 216–218; scheduled maintenance, 192; scheduled service, 86; warranty, 169–170; and winter storage, 195–196
Coast to Coast Resorts, 19
Cold-weather precautions, 68; heating the RV interior, 70–71; protecting the RV, 68–70; water tanks and internal plumbing, 68–69, 71–72
Computers. *See also* E-mail, Internet, Websites; accessories and supplies, 64–65; deciding whether to bring, 63; desktop, 63–64; and e-mail, 128; internet access, 42–43; internet appliances, 125–126; laptop, 63–64, 143–144; personal digital assistants, 126–127, 129, 142; powering in RVs, 43–44, 64
Continued service plans, 170–172
County parks, 76

Digital cameras, 98
Directories and guides; campgrounds, 15–16; interstate exits, 24–25; mountains, 25–26; truck stops, 24
DIRECTV, 56, 57
Discount cards, 21–22
Discount stores, 23–24
DISH Network, 56, 57–58
Documents. *See* Manuals and documents
Driving tips, 130; avoiding commuting hours, 132; cell phone use, 131–132; copilot/navigator, 131–132, 147; drive-through facilities, 134; filling the right tanks, 133–134; going off-road, 135–136; hours per day, 130; lane changes, 132; narrow roads, 137; New York City, 137–138; overdrive, 132; overhead clearance, 131, 134, 136; parking, 131; reasonable schedules, 132; refueling, 132, 133; sharing, 131; stopping time and distance, 130–131; stops, 131; tight clearances, 131
Dry camping, 36

E-mail; appliances (acoustic coupler), 124–125, 126, 129; appliances (plug-in), 123–124, 125, 126, 129; assessing desired technology level, 128–129; via cell phone, 122–123; via global satellite communicators, 127–128; via internet appliances, 125–126, 129; via laptop or desktop computer, 128; via personal digital assistants, 126–127, 129, 142; via phone, 120–122

EAS. *See* Emergency Alert System

Electric hookup, 154–155

Electric step maintenance, 185

Electrical systems; preventive maintenance, 187; preventive maintenance checklist, 217

Emergency Alert System, 60–61

Entertainment centers, 58

Equipment, 22–24

Escapees RV Club, 17

eXitSource 2001, 24–25

Extended warranty services, 170–172

Family Campers and RVers, 17

Family Motor Coach Association, 16, 17, 139

Family Travel Trailer Association, 17

FCRV. *See* Family Campers and RVers

Flying J R.V. RealValue Club, 21

FMCA. *See* Family Motor Coach Association

Furnace maintenance, 190–191

"Gas matches," 98

Global positioning satellite systems, 147–148; high-end (installed), 146–147; low-cost (laptop), 143–144; mid-range (handheld or portable), 144–146; powering, 142–143

Golden Eagle, Age, and Access Passports, 74

Good Sam, 16, 17, 34–35, 139–140

GPS systems. *See* Global positioning satellite systems

Great RV Trips, 33–34

Group travel, 34–35

Guide to Free Campgrounds, 15

Guides. *See* Directories and guides

Highways magazine, 16

Holding tanks; draining, 162; service, 134–135, 160, 162, 163; treating, 163; and winter storage, 199

Home security, 99. *See also* Mail; canceling services, 100; "house angel," 100, 102; inside setup, 101–102; law enforcement and security agencies, 100–101; outside setup and services, 102; pets and plants, 101; telephone service, 99–100; utilities, 102

Hot water heater; maintenance, 186; site setup and take-down, 157

Information sources, 14

Insurance; Canada and Mexico, 78, 81; health and dental, 66–67; and road service, 168; RV, 166–167

Internet. *See also* Computers, E-mail, Web-sites; access, 42–43; appliances, 125–126; banking, 105; service providers, 45–46

Interstate exit guides, 24–25

Jacks, 95; preventive maintenance checklist, 217; and winter storage, 196

Kampgrounds of America, 16; KOA Value Kard, 21

KOA. *See* Kampgrounds of America

KOA Directory and Road Atlas, 21

KVH TracVision dish antennas, 57, 58

Laundry, 61–63

Loading, 90–91; checklist, 91, 219

Local transportation, 47–48

Mail. *See also* E-mail; forwarding service, 118–119, 129; handling options, 117; hold service, 117–118, 129; private mail services, 119–120

Maintenance. *See* Preventive maintenance, Scheduled maintenance, Service

Manuals and documents, 174; chassis, 176; generic repair and maintenance, 177–178; obtaining replacements, 178; organizing, 178–179; power train, 176; RV manufacturer, 175–176; systems and accessories, 177

Manufacturers; manuals and documents, 175–176; user groups, 18; and warranty service, 169–170

Maps, 139; mapping and routing software, 141–142; mapping services, 139–141

Medical concerns, 65; dental insurance, 66–67; health insurance, 66; medical evacuation and assistance, 66, 172–173; prescriptions, 67–68; service providers, 65

Mexico, 77, 80; additional liability insurance, 81; drinking water, 82–83; groceries, 82; guns, 81–82; money exchange, 82; repairs and maintenance, 80–81; touring, 80

Military RV, Camping & Rec Areas Around the World, 16

Money. *See* Banking and money

Mountain Directory East [and West] for Truckers, RV, and Motorhome Drivers, 25–26

Mountain guides, 25–26

National Oceanic and Atmospheric
    Administration, 60–61
National parks, 73; discounted entrance
    fees, 74; websites, 73–74
NOAA. See National Oceanic and
    Atmospheric Administration

Overhead clearance, 131, 134, 136

Parks. See County parks, National parks,
    State parks
Parts, 22–24
Passport America, 21
PDAs. See Personal digital assistants
Personal digital assistants, 126–127, 129;
    and trip routing information, 142
Plumbing, 151; cold-weather precautions,
    68–69, 71–72; holding tanks, 134–135,
    160, 162, 163; sewer hookup, 152–153;
    water hookup, 150–152
PocketMail, 124–125
Polarity testers, 96
Power train; extended warranty, 171;
    manuals and documents, 176; preventive
    maintenance checklist, 215; scheduled
    maintenance, 192–193; scheduled
    service, 86, 87–88; warranty, 169–170;
    and winter storage, 195
President's Club, 21
Preventive maintenance, 180; air-
    conditioning system, 190; awnings, 190;
    batteries, 184; checklists, 215–218; coach
    exterior sidewall, 188; compared with
    scheduled, 181–182; defined, 180; electric
    step, 185; electrical systems, 187; finding
    information on, 182; fluid levels, 183;
    furnace, 190–191; hot water heater, 186;
    refrigerator, 190–191; roof, 189; safety
    items, 186–187; self-done or shop,
    180–181; slideout and leveling system,
    186; stove, 190–191; tire and wheel
    assemblies, 183–184; TV and satellite
    dish antennas, 184–185; water system,
    185; windshield and wipers, 187–188

Refrigerators and coolers, 54–55
Repairs. See also Preventive maintenance,
    Service; manuals and documents,
    177–178; Mexico, 80–81
Resort websites, 27–28
Rest Area Guide, 25

Returning home, 162; cleaning and
    maintenance checklist, 162–163; draining
    holding tanks, 162; filling propane tank,
    162; fuel stabilizer, 163; securing the RV,
    163; treating holding tanks, 163
Road atlases, 139, 147
Road service, 167–168
Roof maintenance, 189
RV Overnighters Association, 17
RV Repair and Maintenance Manual,
    178, 182

Safety ; preventive maintenance of
    equipment, 186–187; considerations,
    38–39; equipment, 52–54, 93–95; general
    five-minute check, 130; heaters and
    stoves, 70; preventive maintenance
    checklist, 217
Satellite TV, 56–58, 79; preventive
    maintenance, 184–185; setup, 157–158
Scheduled maintenance, 191; chassis,
    192–193; coach and related systems,
    192; power train, 192–193; and warranty,
    191, 193
Screen rooms, 59
Service, 22–24, 84; chassis and power train
    scheduled service, 86, 87–88; checking
    tires, 87, 94; checking towing equip-
    ment, 88; coach scheduled service, 86;
    documents, 88; fluid and air checks, 132;
    holding tanks, 134–135, 160, 162, 163;
    prescheduling, 39; pretrip, 87–88;
    preventive maintenance, 86–87;
    providers, 84–86; road and towing,
    167–168; tire, 168; and warranty
    coverage, 84; websites, 29–30
Sewer hookup, 152–153
Site setup and take-down, 149; awnings,
    158; cable TV hookup, 155; electric
    hookup, 154–155; positioning the RV,
    149–150; satellite TV, 157–158; sewer
    hookup, 152–153; slideouts, 156–157;
    stabilizers (levelers), 155–156; stove and
    hot water heater, 157; take-down
    checklist, 158–161; telephone hookup,
    155; TV antenna, 158; water hookup,
    150–152
Slideouts, 156–157; preventive
    maintenance, 186; preventive
    maintenance checklist, 217
Snake lights, 93
Stabilizers (levelers), 155–156; maintenance,
    186

State parks, 74–75; websites and phone numbers, 75–76, 200–214
Storage space, 89–90
Stoves; preventive maintenance, 190–191; safety, 70, 191; site setup and take-down, 157; and soot, 191
Street Atlas USA, 141, 143
Streets & Trips, 141, 143
Sunscreens, 59
Supplies and equipment, 22–24, 92; eliminating, 91; hookup items, 95–97; housekeeping and miscellaneous items, 98; jacks, 95; recreation and leisure items, 97–98; safety equipment, 93–95; tools, 92–93; websites, 29–30

Telephone; answering machines and services, 115; campground hookup, 155; cellular phones, 112–114, 129; e-mail via cell phone, 122–123; e-mail via phone, 120–122; long distance calling cards, 116–117, 129; pay phones, 115; prepaid calling cards, 115–116, 129; regular phones, 114–115; satellite telephones, 117; service options while away, 99–100; two-way pagers, 114
Television and TV sets, 55–58. *See also* Satellite TV; antennas, 158; campground cable hookup, 155; Canada, 79; preventive maintenance, 184–185; satellite setup, 157–158
Tires; checking, 87, 94; jacks, 95; preventive maintenance, 183–184; service, 168; spare, 52–53, 95; and winter storage, 196
Towing (vehicles or trailers); auto trailers, 51–52; combined gross weight rating, 49; determining capability, 48–49; difficulties, 48; emergency equipment, 53–54; spare tires, 52–53, 95; tow bars, 49–50; tow dollies, 50–51
Towing service, 167–168
Trailer Life Directory, 15
Trailer Life RV Campground Finder CD-ROM, 141
Trans-Canada Highway exit guides, 24
Traveler's checks, 104
Trip Book, 39–40
Trip planning, 31–32; choosing destinations, 32–34; group travel, 34–35; mapping and routing software, 141–142; mapping services, 139–141; planning each stop, 35–36; reservations and cancellations, 36–37; road atlases, 139, 147; routing considerations, 37–38; RV library, 40–42; safety considerations, 38–39; service scheduling, 39; Trip Book, 39–40; trip routing services, 139–140; websites, 30, 139–140
TripMaker, 141, 143
Truck stop guides, 24

User groups, 16–17; manufacturers', 18; open to the general public, 17; private campground memberships, 19–21; relative advantages, 18–19; restricted membership, 18; websites, 27

Voltage meters, 96

Warranty, 169–170; extended, 170–172; and scheduled maintenance, 191, 193; and service, 84
Washer/dryers, 62–63
Water hookup, 150–152
Water pressure regulators, 97
Water system; fresh water antifreeze, 198; maintenance, 185; preventive maintenance checklist, 216; and winter storage, 197–198
Weather reports, 59–61
Websites, 26–27. *See also* Computers, E-mail, Internet; campgrounds and resorts, 27–28; miscellaneous, 28–29; national parks, 73–74; supplies, service, and maintenance, 29–30; state parks, 75–76, 200–214; trip routing and navigation, 30; user groups, 27
Wheel assembly maintenance, 183–184
Windshield and wipers; preventive maintenance, 187–188; preventive maintenance checklist, 217–218
Winegard satellite dishes, 56–57, 58
Winter storage of RV, 194–195; and coach, 195–196; and engine, 195; and fresh water antifreeze, 198; and fresh water system, 197–198; and holding tanks, 199; and power train, 195; and tires, 196
Woodall's Campground Directories, 15
Woodall's RV Owners Handbook, 178

Yogi Bear's Jellystone Park Camp-Resorts, 16, 22